Stuff It!

A Wicked Approach To Dieting

Sarah-Kate Lynch

HarperCollins *Publishers New Zealand*

First published 1997
HarperCollins*Publishers (New Zealand) Limited*
P.O. Box 1, Auckland

ISBN 1 86950 258 2

Cover photo by Craig Owen
Cover designed by Mike McHugh
Designed and typeset by ArcherDesign
Printed by Sino Publishing House, Hong Kong

Dedicated to our friend, the elastic waistband.

ACKNOWLEDGEMENTS

I'd like to thank all my family and friends for being such good cooks, I mean sorts, and my husband Mark for all his love and support, and for laughing when I show him my wobbly bits.

Contents

– 1 –
So a fat is a thing you wear on your head, right?

In which a young girl discovers the cruel truth about wobbly thighs and bikinis and exposes the down side of having three boyfriends at once

I'VE LONG SUSPECTED that the twinkle in my father's eye that eventually turned out to be me was, in fact, originally aimed at a piece of my grandmother's chocolate caramel slice. Well, it was the best in all of Central Otago, after all. And how else can you explain a battle with corpulence that has spanned more than three decades and seen a grown (or should that be growing) woman lose and gain the equivalent of approximately four and a half Kylie Minogues?

There must be more to it than the fact that if it's deep-fried, I like it, and if it's exercise, I tried that once and it didn't work. Surely there's *someone* I can blame and therefore can track up hill and down dale, through rain, hail, sleet and snow, at my peril, against all odds and kill, therefore discovering the elixir of svelteness. Or is that a movie with Sylvester Stallone?

Stuff It!

Because if the answer to eternal size 10-ness is to simply eat less and move more, frankly, I'm a lard-arse for the long haul.

Of course, in the 60s — when I was born — it was all the rage to have enormous offspring. In my mind I see Plunket rooms the country over full with row upon row of slender, stylish mums in Doris Day cinched-waist dresses and stilettos straining under the weight of their enormous babies.

'Please, please, let mine be off the chart,' they would each have silently prayed, while surreptitiously stuffing barley sugars into their junior giants' mouths in a desperate bid to beat the other mothers in the race for the chubbiest.

How tragic for the Doris Day sent fleeing in tears from the room with the words 'Smaller Than Average' stamped forever on her baby's Plunket book and a leaflet like *How To Make Your Breast Milk Work For You* stuffed in her purse.

But how enchanting for the Doris singled out and congratulated on her acceptance into the Michelin hall of fame for her dedication to corpulence in a minor. Never mind that you can't tell whether it's a boy or a girl, or in fact a small, smocked country.

I suspect another motivational factor for encouraging roly-polliness in babies of the time was to cut down the incidence of lesions and contusions on said roly-pollies should a nasty car accident occur. In those days, child restraints would have been laughed out of the coffee mornings as the work of a mad scientist because every woman knew that should she slam her stilettos on the brakes in a hurry those round little balls lying loosely on the back seat would just bounce around, happily sucking on a rusk and chuckling to themselves as they thought dreamily of sago and junket pudding (bleeeeuuurrrrggggh). Why, a girl had to keep the back windows closed should one of those balls just darn well bounce right out of the Morris Minor and down the street, for jiminy's sake!

Actually, I was initially something of a disappointment in the roly-poly stakes. Hey, you, pick yourself up off the floor and quit laughing! In fact, slap your thigh one more time and I'll banish you straight to the epilogue.

I was born three weeks early (the first and last time I was early for anything) and weighed a mere six pounds five ounces (the first and last time I weighed a mere anything). There must have been a few tense moments in the Plunket rooms for the first couple of weeks, by jingoes! But I'm happy to say that right then and there I began an attempt to eat my way to the Larger Than Average part of the graph to save my family from the embarrassment that otherwise would have surely ruined them. And in a strange twist, I'm still headed for that part of the graph. Ten points for consistency, the cheers go up. I may have toyed a couple of times with Goal Range, and once even slipped into Below Average, but that was only for about half an hour and the result of several hundred diet pills (see chapter 5) so it doesn't really count.

As a toddler I would describe myself as pleasantly plump. Actually, I'm still describing myself as that, but at least I'm not wearing a smocked dress with matching knickers any more. Well, I don't care what they told you at work, I'm not. I certainly had no problem at all with my pleasantly plumpness during my kindergarten years, although I've often suspected my lifelong revulsion of exercise may stem back to hours spent doing the twist with our kindy teacher Miss Whatever. I've always been more of a Sit On The Mat And You Too sort of a person. I also suspect that my childhood habit of eating the dough rather than moulding it into interesting shapes may be responsible for the fact that I would still rather eat the dough than mould it into interesting shapes should dough suddenly become a part of everyday modern life for a woman in her 30s.

Neither did porkiness play a huge part in my first few years at St Dominic's Primary School, although the brown gymslip never did a thing for any mortal but perhaps, in particular, me.

I do still bear the shame of stealing 50 cents, though, and

spending it all on sweeties at the Maori (pronounced Maree) Hill dairy. Actually, I never meant to take the money but when Miss Whatever asked whose it was and I put my hand up to say it must belong to someone from the other primer who'd come in to our classroom for Religion she came over and plopped it into my outstretched hand before I could open my mouth, and for some reason, words failed me. Had I known it was the first and only time words would fail me I would probably have made more of it, but never mind.

Needless to say it was big bifter time in the sweetie department at the dairy on the way home, but my fatal mistake was to share my good fortune with a boy from down the road who obviously caved in the second he got home (never mind torture) and told his mother it was me what provided the Rollos. Naturally, she was on the phone lickety-split to Mrs Lynch and by the time I got home chock-a-block full of sherbet and liquorice allsorts there was a right old hoo-ha going on.

Any long-term plans I had of forging out a career as an embezzler went down the gurgler then and there, and I still struggle not to fess up at the counter when I've been given too much change. OK, OK, I said I *struggle* not to fess up, but I'm happy to report it's a struggle I manage to overcome.

Already, as a five-year-old, the point of sport was eluding me. The only two even vaguely sporty things I can remember is being whacked in the scongo by a baseball bat and having an egg-sized lump on my forehead as a result. Hey, maybe that's what I can blame for my addiction to fried food! Maybe the bit of my brain that says pies and sausage rolls and fish and chips and salt and vinegar crisps should only be eaten in moderation had the bejeezus squashed out of it that day with that one fell swoop, leaving me a shadow of my former self. Err, make that two shadows.

And the other vaguely sporty thing? Hm, it seems to have escaped me. Maybe there was only one after all. Is it any wonder

I never represented our country at rhythmic gymnastics? Oh, now I remember. The other thing that put me off sport was my little sister vomiting on the carousel at Carisbrook while Dad coached rugby.

I can't actually remember the exact point at which I worked out that Larger Than Average was, in fact, what I was and an altogether bad thing to be, but I'm pretty sure it had something to do with swimming togs (leastways, that's when I'm most reminded of it these days).

Thankfully, being brought up in Dunedin, swimming togs were not often called for, although Mum and Dad did take my brother, sister and I to swimming lessons at the Moana Pool. In fact, it was Duncan Laing, trainer of Olympic gold medallist Danyon Loader, who taught the little Lynches to freestyle. I'm sure he'd be thrilled to learn that we've turned into a family of complete and utter lard-arses who wouldn't swim from one side of the bath to the other without spending two weeks trying to get booked on the ferry first.

I don't know if Duncan's methods have changed at all in recent years, but in those days he had a very straightforward technique. If you made it to the end of the pool without embarrassing yourself in any way, you got a Crunchie bar. But if you took a wrong turn or sank to the bottom you were bonked on the head with a long wooden pole operated poolside by Duncan dressed in a string singlet.

Needless to say, I have never quite gotten over my insatiable desire for Crunchie bars, and I get a lot of headaches.

I'm also prone to taking out a carving knife and plunging it into the chest of anyone wearing a string singlet and bearing a wooden pole, but thankfully that doesn't happen so often these days.

Anyway, back to swimming togs. I do recall at the age of about seven talking Mum into making me a bikini, which is the only time in my life I've ever worn one and that has nothing whatsoever to do with the Paraparaumu Petition of 1982, thank you for asking.

My bikini had a blue and white cotton top that buttoned at the back so you had to ask the lady next to you in the changing rooms to undo it for you (and by the way, lady, I have since found out that sucking your plaits does not lead to hair growing in your lungs, but thanks for the tip) and a navy blue bottom made of towelling.

Quite fetching while sitting perched on the edge of the kiddies pool at Moana, the bikini bottoms proved to have something of a fatal flaw which revealed itself the first time they were worn to the beach.

Lined with a porous fabric, the bottoms filled up with an extra-ordinary load of sand of which they could not be rid, and hence gave the sporter the unfortunate appearance of having a very bulky, low-slung bottom, the likes of which would prompt gasps of admiration and 'look at the buns on that thing' from even the heftiest Hottentot.

Anyway, the bikini became a bad look and was ditched. Had I known then that it was the last bikini I would ever wear I probably would have grinned and bore the sagging bottom. Actually, come to think of it, I'm doing that anyway, only without the bikini. True story. Never mind.

My eighth-birthday recollection combines the Moana Pool and one of my first food obsessions, although I can't remember what swimming togs I was wearing. (For some strange reason I can remember that a girl called Teresa Gutteridge who had goose-berries growing in her back yard gave me a pink handbag. I wonder what happened to that handbag? I wonder what happened to Teresa Gutteridge?)

Our family was about to move to Auckland so it was a partic-ularly momentous occasion and one of the last chances ever to see my Dunedin friends. For this reason, I was allowed to indulge in the passion of the time, the ice cream cake. What a gyp it would seem in these days of triple chocolate peppermint chip with Frangelico goulash but believe me, back then, an ice cream cake was as good as it got. I mean, we're talking strictly vanilla at home. We're talking Neapolitan was a big deal. We're talking only the rich folk got to sample hokey pokey.

So, with the passage of time, this ice cream cake returns to my memory as something so big that Donny Osmond or David Cassidy or even Tom Jones could jump out of it and… do whatever an eight-year-old wants a heart-throb to do with them. Eat ice cream cake, probably.

(I was deemed slightly peculiar at the time for my fixation with Tom Jones and was even allowed to stay up late to watch his TV show, once we got a TV. I just loved the way he snogged someone behind a flimsy screen then came out on to the stage to have his own body weight in industrial strength knickers hiffed at him from screaming fans. Did they take their knickers off when he was snogging, especially for hurling purposes? Or did they bring a nice clean pair of extras from home? Or was there a man in the orchestra pit with a giant selection from Woolworths who came up in the credits as Knicker Wrangler? I talked to Tom Jones on the phone a couple of years ago setting up an interview and I tell you, my affection for him had dwindled over the decades but two minutes on the phone and my own knickers were practically working their way off of their own accord.) However, I digress.

It was also at about this age that my lifelong love of fish and chips developed. Being Catholics, we weren't allowed to eat meat on a Friday, although I didn't spot this until I was about 22 and up until then thought it merely a happy coincidence. Mum and Dad would eat fish pie, the very sight of which can still make me rush to the lav retching, but we kids were usually — unless we had been particularly cruel to each other or them — allowed to have a friend home after school and get amongst the f and c with all the alacrity we could muster, which was quite a lot, plus tomato sauce which, being a fish and chip purist, I personally feel spoils them but I know I am vastly outnumbered here so I won't go on although you really should try them without a couple of times and then see what you think. It used to cost 20 cents for two pieces of fish or two hot dogs and a scoop of chips. My, how times have changed.

Of course, fish and chips have been completely ruined for me now after an exposé on television revealed that they were the most fattening thing a person could eat — more fattening even than anything in the world apart from, possibly, deep-fried Mars Bars, currently all the rage in the Outer Hebrides or some other Bermuda Triangle of low cholesterol. Anyway, it's been a year since fish and chips passed my lips and I still dream of them every now and then. Never with tomato sauce.

But getting back to discovering that fat is a bad thing, which happened nearly 30 years ago. It was at the Moana Pools (again — what is it with this place?) that I first noticed that some girls' thighs joined together at the top and some seemed widely spaced apart. I don't think I was particularly pervy in noticing this, it's just that I was investigating another stunning revelation at the time which was that really pretty girls also had bottoms, which up until the Moana Pools changing rooms I had thought not to be the case, as the result of a small misunderstanding in the playground one lunchtime with a friend who claimed to know how babies were born and other details of Down Below.

Now as far as these girls who had big spaces between the tops of their thighs were concerned, I actually felt sorry for them because, being from Otago, I imagined this would cause a sharp drop in their body temperature should the southerly wind whip through. I was also vaguely concerned because I knew in horses it was a sign that they were good jumpers but I couldn't quite imagine how this would translate to eight-year-old girls.

It never for a moment occurred to me that the chubbier among us were in fact the ones to be pitied. Why would it? I mean at this stage I had three boyfriends all called Michael, for goodness' sake.

Stuff It!

There was nothing wrong with my thighs, missus.

Like the aforementioned bikini, had I known it would be the last time in my life I would ever have three boyfriends at once I would have made more of it, I'm sure. Frankly, it's been enough trouble having one at a time ever since, let alone a trio all handily called the same thing to avoid embarrassment in later years, should one's mind become confused during the interesting bits if you know what I mean, and I think you do.

Actually, one of the Michaels was quite advanced now that I look back on it. We used to pash in his mother's wardrobe for hours at a time — with tongues, do you mind — while his hands wandered down inside the back of my knickers and squeezed my bottom. I always wondered what that was about, and in fact I still do and certainly wouldn't countenance putting up with it these days, not that there's room in my knickers for a set of wandering hands anyway; heavens, I can hardly fit my bottom in them.

One of the other Michaels had a stunning doll collection and a penchant for those heart-shaped lollies sporting messages like 'I love you' and 'best friend', three for a cent if I remember rightly, and most generous he was with them, too.

I can't remember much about the other Michael apart from the fact that he rarely spoke. I think he was my favourite.

The point is, not one of these Mikes was fazed by a pudgy knee or a wobbly thigh, so at which point exactly were they made aware that bigger might be better but thin is in, just answer me that one, eh?

Do the bigger boys in long pants pull them aside on the way home from school one night and drag them into the bushes for a bizarre initiation ceremony where cellulite is reviled as the work of the devil and flab is exposed as being akin to losing at conkers? One day I'll get to the bottom of that mystery, even if I have to have a son to do so.

Shortly after the great ice cream cake birthday of 1970, our family moved to Auckland, to a house near the beach at Mission

Bay where we would go swimming after school — a concept it took us quite a while to grasp having lived in Dunedin for so long.

There were two gorgeous, dark, swarthy twins who were in my class at my new school, St Ignatius (patron saint of broken legs if memory serves me correctly), and while neither of these twins was called Michael I fancied either/or as a replacement for my affections.

But sitting on the beach one afternoon in my pale green velour togs, it was cruelly revealed to me by one of the twins that I was, in fact, fat, and unlikely ever to get a boyfriend at all. In fact, I think he said something like 'Hey, you're fat, you'll never get a boyfriend. Want to play knuckle bones?'

Excuse me, but how could this be? Me? *Fat?* OK, I remember thinking, maybe a little on the outside I'll give you that, but on the inside I was someone who was used to having three boy-friends all called Michael so don't come round here with your fat jibes and taunts of a lonely life spent entirely on the shelf, sonny Jim, because it don't hold no truck with me, no sirreee. Well, I remember thinking something a bit like that; all right, not much like that but that's what I'm thinking now — so sue me!

Anyway, once I had thrashed both twins four times each at knuckle bones and derided them for both still being only on Level 2 spelling I went home and asked Mum what a diet was and if I put one on (I've since learned that you have to go on one rather than have it go on you) how long would it take me to get thin.

'Oh, about a year,' she said casually, as she lifted the baby out of the car, stopped my sister from giving her doll the Gidget haircut for the forty-fourth time and helped my brother with his maths.

A year? Were my ears deceiving me? It had only taken two min-utes to find out that I was fat. How could it take a year to be thin again? In a year's time I would be nine — that was inconceivable.

I decided then and there to start my diet the next day — and

I've pretty much been deciding that ever since.

By the way, after years of research I have recently discovered that there is no down side to having three boyfriends at once.

- 2 -
And they call it puppy fa-a-a-at (thanks Donny)

In which ponchos get the marching boot and rompers are revealed as the work of the devil

ONCE I REALISED I was fat, life pretty much went downhill from there. Thank goodness I'd had eight years luxuriating in my innocence, although I guess these days that would be called denial. I can't believe the recent reports that six-year-old girls around the world are now suffering from anorexia. In my book (which, in a happy coincidence, this is) if you can't spell it, you can't have it. Now, if more people stuck to that the world would be full of better spellers and fewer anorexics, and bouillabaisse sales would go through the roof. Personally, I have lived nearly all my life by the spelling/eating maxim and I can happily report that my enormous appetite is outdone only by my ability to spell, even under pressure. In my constant quest for moderation, however, I have tempered the spell it/eat it rule with that other great maxim, never eat anything bigger than your head. I have cheated slightly here, I confess, by encouraging my hair to be curly at all times but especially when eating, and by assuming that it means never eat any one item bigger than your head because, of course, an evening's fare when rolled together and sculpted the right way (which thankfully rarely happens) could quite easily outweigh the average scongo.

For instance, remember the model who died after starving herself for two days and then going on an eating binge? The contents of her stomach revealed she had eaten a whole cabbage (no doubt bigger than her head), several meat pies, a packet of chocolate macaroons, one and a half loaves of bread, a dozen Christmas mince pies and a packet of Oddfellows. Frankly, anyone who eats a dozen Christmas mince pies is dicing with the dark side, but who didn't read that list of the contents of her last meal and think, There now, see, if she'd just stuck to eating things smaller than her head she'd still be alive today, on a drip in some anorexic ward? Hmmm?

My point, and I do have one, is that there is no such thing as an original line. Oh, no, that wasn't it at all. My point is that at six years old the last thing you should be worrying about is what you are eating and what size it is making you. Yeez, save that torture for when you're a teenager! At six you should simply be making sure that you are, in fact, the centre of your parents' universe, and that you do have more Barbie accessories than your best friend and her seven-year-old cousin from Sydney, you know, the one with the leather miniskirt and frosty tipped hair.

Although I am not a great fan of blaming the fad of the time on the shortcomings of a generation, Barbie probably has to take a sliver of responsibility when it comes to today's six-year-old anorexics. I mean, you don't have to be able to spell 'big tits' to realise that Barbie has a set the likes of which even the pope himself would like to put his head between and go 'wibba, wibba wibba'. Hasn't someone somewhere done a study that revealed if Barbie was alive and breathing she'd actually have to keep most of her internal organs in her lovely-handbag-and-matching-hat because there is simply no room in her torso? I'm sure I remember reading that. When I was six, only the rich kids who also got to go to Fiji in the holidays and had colour televisions had Barbies. The rest of us were stuck with Cindy, who was rather more stockily arranged and whose bosoms have left no impression on me whatsoever, but her hair, whoa, now there's another story. If today's six-year-olds are starving themselves to death in a bid to emulate Barbie I can only thank the heavens that my generation didn't take to wearing their mousy brown nylon hairdos in a Cindy-style birds' nest.

Anyway, getting back to my horrifying discovery as an eight-year-old that far from looking like either of the Hayley Millses in the *Parent Trap*, I was, in fact, a porker, this started my hate-hate relationship with clothes. I still face the same uneasy struggle with my wardrobe even though I now realise that being generously proportioned isn't worse than having no arms, no legs, no head and buck teeth, as I thought it was then.

I was not helped in my new-found corpulence to be right smack in the middle of the micro-mini and hot pants fad. (In a cruel twist I'm right back smack in the middle of it again now, but that's retro for you, isn't it?) Thankfully, Mum was not silly enough to bow to my pleas for a micro-mini, but I have a nasty feeling in the pit of my stomach that she may have acquiesced to the hot pants — or perhaps that was for my sister, Anna. It's not as unusual as you might think for me to be confused about things that happened to her and things that happened to me because although I have always been two years older (yep, that's pretty much how it works) we have always looked so much the same that we could pass for twins, and until we each left home we separately assumed we were both called Sarah-Anna because that's what our parents usually seemed to call us, which was probably not the best way of developing our separate psyches but at least assured them a 100 per cent strike rate. Later, when our baby sister came along, our names were all lengthened to Sarah-Anna-Rachael.

So Anna may have had the hot pants, not me, and if she did they were purple and also if she did it signalled the end of us being dressed in identical clothes which was not only great for us (the end of it I mean) but easier for those trying to identify us.

The identical outfits I particularly remember were pink gingham smock dresses that we wore with red leather shoes and matching kilts made specially for us by Mr Hootsmon in Dunedin; these we wore with twin sets I am hoping at least differed in colour. The word 'biscuit' keeps popping into my mind so it could be that was the colour of the twinset I was forced to wear, or it could be I feel like a biscuit, I guess I'll never know unless I have that biscuit. Nope, you see now the words 'salt and vinegar crisps' are popping into my mind so I guess biscuit was the colour of the twinset after all.

Understandably, I have been physically repelled by biscuits since the one I had about a nanosecond ago, but even more so I have been repelled by pink gingham smock dresses ever since the 60s, although I am sure they were all the rage at the time (please God pink gingham smocks don't do a retro on us). I do hold some small fascination for things tartan, as long as they are rugs. And I strongly suspect that were I tragically wounded in, say, a terrible knitting accident that left me perfectly normal in most respects but reliant on my mother for getting dressed in the morning, I would be wearing kilts and twinsets as we speak.

It was my great desire at this stage, largely because of the uniform, to become a marching girl. Something about those buttoned jackets, twirling mini skirts and white boots really appealed (just as well I wasn't growing up in Nazi Germany), but no matter how much I begged Mum, she would not have a bar of it and I've meant to ask her many times over the past 20 years or so why it was so out of the question but I keep forgetting.

It's possible I wouldn't have been much chop at the synchronised side of being a marching girl anyway, given that over the years I have failed to develop a team player whatsiname. Anyway, I was recently put off the whole idea while producing Sharon Crosbie's morning show on National Radio when she and I became entranced by the inappropriateness of a male marching team manager who seemed to pay more than a passing interest in the way the girls 'panties' would show when they twirled their new skirts. The 'panties' were made of gold fabric and by the sounds of it, what these 'panties' couldn't do was barely worth mentioning. I've no doubt there was nothing sinister about his enthusiasm for the 'panties' but it did seem odd for a grown man to show such robust glee in a spangly uniform, and our mirth was hardly dampened by the fact that the marching team was sponsored by and named after a well-known brand of dog food.

Getting back to clothes I was cruelly kept from, however, ponchos were the other thing back in those days. Other girls at school had ponchos in every colour of the rainbow, but not the Lynch girls, no sirree. I think we finally got identical navy blue towelling versions to wear at the beach — that's right, the return of the blue towelling. Maybe they were fashioned together using off-cuts from the disastrous bikini bottoms.

Now I realise that ponchos are only worn by feminists who smoke pipes and write books and live in remote spots where they craft cellphone holders out of dried seaweed to swap with tourists for large amounts of Uncle Igor's Famous Falling Over Water, so I'm dead happy I never developed a fixation with them after all (ponchos, I mean).

Actually, a poncho, had it not been taken over by the likes of the aforementioned, would realistically be practical clothing for anyone outside the regular shape, because once you move more than a few pounds outside the norm, clothing becomes something which is aimed at disguising you rather than enhancing you.

Hence, by the age of nine I felt that shorts were something to be avoided and sleeveless tops belonged in the same cupboard, i.e. not mine. While some overweight people can happily wear the fashion of the time and not worry that a bulge protrudes here or a gentle roll there, I have dedicated a lifetime to not looking as fat as I actually am, and I have to say I'm not half bad at it.

I was helped in this endeavour by being forced to go to Catholic schools where a uniform was compulsory and even Protestants (who we felt sorry for because we were told they were worshipping their own god when really it was only the Catholic God who counted) knew back then that absolutely everybody looked like a bag of shit in those outfits (especially the ones in brown), so it was quite hard to determine who actually was one or not.

At St Dominic's in Dunedin it was brown and came with a hat. At St Ignatius in Auckland it was blue with grey socks, do you mind. No hat. At Sacred Heart Intermediate in Wellington it was green, and at St Mary's School for Sluts and Unmarried Mothers, as I so kindly used to call it, it was grey and white saved only by a black jersey and black blazer, though in the third form it came with a hat and gloves which was like a permission for every other school pupil who caught the Johnsonville unit to town to taunt, harass and desecrate our outfits and really, who could blame them?

All of these Catholic uniforms had one horrifying feature in common — the romper, or in plural, and there was no doubt that that's what they came in, rompers. For the uninitiated, rompers are a pantaloon worn by young Catholic girls when partaking in the playing of sporting activities. They are gathered at the waist, and again at the top of each thigh. They are the most unattractive garment in the universe and would be evidence alone for aliens to blast us into another stratosphere should they find rompers being worn on their descent to earth. It is impossible for even the most slender girl to look attractive in rompers. They are a cruel mistake.

I suspect now that rompers were invented to make jiggling

Catholic girls look uninviting to even the most deviated pervert caught hanging around the playground ('Oh, I'm sorry, Father Brown, I thought you were someone else'). I am convinced that my lifelong hatred of all things sporting hinges on the fear of rompers that was drummed into me from the moment I realised pudgy thighs weren't as good as the firm, hard ones.

In terms of my theory that clothes could be used to cover the flaws in your body, rompers took no prisoners. You couldn't lengthen them. You couldn't loosen them. Dang, you couldn't even take them out into the middle of the desert and blow them to kingdom come. They were no doubt the result of years of intensive research carried out in the basement of some dark, dank, dingy convent by a coven of scientific nuns whose life mission it was to destroy young girls' desires to run around bouncing alluringly by incarcerating them in the modern equivalent of a chastity belt.

From the age of ten, the very phrase PE struck fear into my thighs and made them wobble. Unnecessarily, I mean. Coupled with my inability to keep my eyes open while a ball was hurtling towards me and a fantastic absence of hand-to-eye coordination, I was a lemon in the eyes of every PE teacher I ever had. Little did they know it was the rompers that sucked my confidence out even before I hit the playground as I slipped them on over my regulation knickers. How could a girl feel good about herself in those things? It's a miracle she could feel anything given the tightness of the elastic (although maybe that was the evil science nuns' intention).

My other phobia of the time that also involved rompers was netball. I have been genetically graced with height and currently stand at around 178 cm which is around 5'10". For this I am now truly grateful (it's especially handy for rock concerts and intimidating short men, usually accountants), but as a chunky ten-year-old it was just something else that wasn't quite normal and meant you always stood at the back in the middle for class photos. How I longed to be one of the midgets sitting cross-legged in the front!

Anyway, the nuns assumed that my height would give me natural grace and skill on the netball court and so every year they would put me in the top team as goalkeeper, possibly the most boring position in the game, definitely the way I played it. Somewhere along the line I had missed out on where the fun in netball actually was, so I stood miserably at the opposition end with one hand flailing around uselessly as goal after goal was scored before my very eyes — the centre and goal attack looking at me with scorn and loathing in theirs.

Every year I would be dropped out of the top team within the first couple of weeks and degraded throughout the system until I eventually ended up in the bottom team playing with the people under five foot, in wheelchairs and with very thick spectacles. I still couldn't stop a goal from being scored to save myself. By the third form, each team member was issued with a wraparound skirt, but by then it was too late. The rompers had rendered me useless forever.

- 3 -
Thank you, Sister, for helping me with my self-esteem

In which you look back over your teenage years and realise you'd kill to be that fat now

AT HIGH SCHOOL I always fancied myself as a sort of Naughtiest Girl In The School, complete with an unruly mop of black curly hair and a history of jolly japes and jaunty jibes the likes of which kept the nuns beside themselves with laughter in the staff room.

Sadly for me, in my first year at St Mary's I was pretty much too scared to even speak let alone keep my classmates hysterical with my jolly hockey sticks humour. Also, my sensible brown pageboy was positively ruly, and I hadn't even heard of home perms then so it was likely to stay that way for some time to come.

Much of my self-consciousness at this stage sprang from the fact that at 12 years old I was much the same height as I am now (unless that shrinking as you're older thing has already started). I seemed to be constantly surrounded by midgets and was always the first person picked out of an assembly of 600 girls to be told to straighten her shoulders. I hate it when that happens. Looking back at photos taken at the time I was not particularly fat. I was not particularly thin either, of course, but it was my general bigness that made me feel uncomfortable.

The rest of my fear sprang directly from the well of Sister Mary Eulalia, my third-form teacher. You know the scary old lady who lives down the street from you when you are little who can strike muck into the underpants of even the staunchest toddler just by exiting her house to put the milk bottles out? Well, times her by a hundred and you have Sister Eulalia.

Lord knows what torture this little woman had been through herself to come up with the methods she used to humiliate and terrorise teenagers into learning French and maths, but man she must have had some practice before she got to us.

One day I was being lulled to sleep by the warmth of the sun being absorbed into my black school jumper. Not paying attention and playing with your pencils were the two biggest crimes in 3E, so in order to avoid the former I started to remove the offending jersey.

'Sarah Lynch, what do you think you are doing,' the poisonous dwarf bellowed, her black eyes twinkling with the joy of another humiliation.

'Taking my jersey off, Sister,' I replied nervously.

'Well, stop it at once.'

You didn't muck around with this woman, believe me, so I started to put the jersey back on again.

'Sarah Lynch, didn't you hear me?' Her voice had a definite nasty edge to it which, even with my head inside my half-on half-off jersey, I could still pick up.

'I'm just putting my jersey back on, Sister.'

'Well, girlie, when I say stop it, I mean stop it — so stop it.'

OK, Sister, if it's that important to you that I complete the lesson with the jersey half on and half off that's fine by me, I'm just a dumb 13-year-old but you've only got yourself to blame if I start wondering about the credibility of Christian kindness displayed in your particular brand of brides of Christ. I mean, really!

This was the kind of crankiness that we newcomers to St Mary's endured for the first year and I must say that while it hardly endeared anyone to the convent as a career choice, it was most unlikely you would get your past and present tenses mixed up in French or forget to do your maths homework.

I did have the chance later on to thank Sister Eulalia for the jumper incident and her other confidence building skills by doing somersaults down the aisle of the convent chapel while her dead body lay open faced in a coffin at the front. That'll learn her.

I suppose if nuns had known about self-esteem back then they might have done things a bit differently (OK, not the nuns but maybe the lay teachers). As it was, they continued their tyrannical rule without which I might have remained a serious student dedicated only to her studies and never having a good haircut.

But early into my fourth form year I realised that being good was for the birds because it was unlikely that you could ever be good enough to be the best, so you may as well have a crack at being bad instead. Don't get me wrong — I was still completely gutless. I didn't have the nerve to wag, or smoke fags, or walk down Hawkstone Street which was out of bounds because of a large flat of ruffians who lived there. But I did sometimes eat in the streets. Yes, it's true. I still do sometimes now, too, although I have to be honest and say it never feels quite right, even if it's just an apple.

The worst thing I probably ever did in all my high school years was push aside the bunsen burners and stand on the desk in the science lab yelling at the teacher that I knew the nuns were desperate for chemistry teachers but they had really scraped the bottom of the barrel when they employed him. It must have hit a raw nerve because he chased me three times around the room without catching me (he must have been very slow) then sentenced me to 300 lines of something like 'I must not accuse the nuns of scraping the bottom of the barrel for chemistry teachers'.

Luckily for me, and thanks to some serious vote fixing, I was class captain at the time and enlisted the help of the whole classroom in completing the punishment. Delegation is a wonderful thing, is it not?

I'm now ashamed to even think of some of the tricks we played on our fourth form teacher, kindly known as Magilla Gorilla, who was probably a bit too kind to be a teaching nun and after the strict regime of Sister Eulalia, something of a pushover. So much so, in fact, that although it was supposed to be the first year that French was taught audio-visually, we hid the extension cord for the tape recorder under a loose floorboard at the back of the room and so managed to go nearly a whole year without hearing a single tape. We would orchestrate it so that one half of the class would start humming, then the other, for a whole hour. No wonder poor Magilla disappeared halfway through the year and was rumoured to have been seen on the same bus as another nun who had long since been thought to travel out to Porirua Hospital every Thursday for shock treatment.

Magilla's replacement was a lay teacher who was great fun, but even she had difficulty controlling us by that stage. This was a class used to spending most of it's time playing gin rummy, after all.

At this time, despite being a terrible show-off constantly seeking the limelight that rightfully belonged to someone else, I was, nevertheless, deeply self-conscious about my body. I felt enormous and, in fact, I was — compared to my closest girlfriends. This is where I needed an older, wiser sister who would say, 'Get with the programme, girlfriend, you need some friends who are fatter than you!'

How it irks me when I look at photos of myself back then that I was so pained about being fat — I'd give my right leg (OK, only the extra bits at the top) to be that fat now. If anything, I should have been worried about my hair. What was it with the 70s? Some of those hairdos make Michael Bolton look well coiffed — the ones where I didn't look like some kind of demented choirboy that is. Yeez, and I was worried about a few extra pounds?

I guess then it wasn't the done thing for friends or parents or definitely siblings to tell you you were OK the way you were. In fact, it's probably not the done thing now, either, but what a difference it would make. I recently went to a wedding where I was reunited with a handful of my closest girlfriends from St Mary's. Despite the intervening 20 or so years we all seemed just the same to me. In fact, when the soundtrack from *Grease* started playing (I'm assuming it was a request by the bride) we all took to the dance floor and it was just like being back at that hideous fifth form social, although now we were not so embarrassed to be dancing with only each other because we knew there was a clutch of bored out of their brains husbands sitting around somewhere, even if they were just rolling their eyes at the recollection of yet another jolly jape.

'My God, you've lost so much weight,' I said to the bride — who was one of three of us at school always on a diet (the third was also ogling the bride's waistline).

'Actually, I haven't,' she said cheerfully. 'Actually, I am exactly the same size I have been since I was 13 — it's just that I always thought I was fat.' Well, what a waste of dieting that was! At least my other friend and I have actually put on weight since then and so we repaired to the back of the room where we lamented the fact that probably the only time in our lives we didn't need to be on diets was when they were all we could think of.

'It was all in our heads,' she said sadly, as the deep-fried finger foods came around again.

Of course, the nuns can hardly be held responsible for our atrocious body images, partly because they were not allowed to mention the word 'body' and partly because I'm pretty sure that confidence-building was seen by the nuns as the work of Beezlebub himself.

Don't get me wrong — we would have been serial dieters no

matter where we went to school. After all, it's not such a bad thing being brought up by the Catholics (although I wouldn't do it to my own children, but then I don't have any and that's only because I'm too scared to have sex in case the ghost of Sister Eulalia appears shouting 'I told you, girlie, stop it, stop it at once,' and next thing you know I'm on the Thursday bus going off for a special electric treat, know what I'm saying?).

Personally, I think being taught a bunch of cobblers by elderly virgins makes you sort out for yourself pretty early on what is true and proper and what is 'Hello! Hello! Anybody in there?' For instance, when a nun in the sixth form explained to we 16-year-olds that a girl who has sex before she is married is known as a prostitute we all just laughed about it gently at lunchtime saying what a silly old duffer she was and obviously no one had pointed out to her that a good percentage of her class were already nobbing their spotty boyfriends, and that to be even a halfway decent prostitute there has to be an exchange of funds and didn't she know that some prostitutes were actually married?

There's also a great kindred spirit among the Catholics. My friend Mike and I often laugh about this and say yes, it was a terrible time and yes, the nuns should mostly have been taken outside and lined up against the jungle gym and shot or at least tickled relentlessly with a feather, and the priests and brothers should have kept their hands in their own pockets, but now when you meet someone new and they reveal they were Catholic once too it's a bit like discovering a new member in your club (none of those funny handshakes, mind, not after what Father X did to cousin Johnny behind the altar wine cupboard). No one I know still goes to church or is a practising Catholic but once you've been tortured by the clergy you've a lifelong bond to other survivors.

I'm not sure if it's a Catholic girls' thing or not but my last couple of years at St Mary's seemed to be largely spent staving off wetting my pants with laughter, and it wasn't just me either. On one occasion, three other girlfriends and I were trying to escape the compound undetected. Being located in central Wellington too close to the lure of the shops and seedy taverns, we had to have a note from our mothers to leave the school grounds at lunchtime.

As we usually didn't want our mothers to know that we were being lured by the shops and seedy taverns, it was a case of forgery or escape, and on this day we chose the latter. Actually, seedy taverns held little allure at that stage (my, how things change!) and in this instance our plan was to buy a box of All-Bran and some milk and eat it in the grounds of Parliament. What a jolly jape!

The best way to escape undetected without proceeding down the evil valley of Hawkstone St was to sneak through the wilderness down beside the tennis courts and climb over a wooden fence that left you on a bushy bank halfway up Molesworth St. Then all you had to do was scramble down a retaining wall and you were out.

Stage one of our plan was successful. We all made it to the fence. The first two got over without incident and then it was my turn. This is where things went horribly wrong. I got halfway over the fence and attempted to jump off the other side when my regulation knickers got caught on a fence paling and refused to release me, so I was left hanging from said fence by elastic of said knickers, a fine testament to their suitability as regulation jobs. Unfortunately for the girl behind me, her finger was trapped between my knickers and the fence, which seemed to be quite uncomfortable for her although I couldn't even feel a tickle. Unfortunately for me, at that exact moment the girl in front of me on the freedom side of the fence let go of a piece of undergrowth which sprang back with alarming speed and hit me right in the clacker. Being helpless with laughter while stuck on a fence with a girlfriend's finger trapped in your knickers and a large foreign bush between your legs is a recipe for loss of bladder control if ever there was one, wouldn't you agree?

Stuff It!

The All-Bran stage was an interesting one, just raising the tone a tad. For me it was at 15 that food really became a problem in terms of fluctuating between stuffing yourself with it or starving yourself of it. My girlfriends and I would often escape with a loaf of bread, some Vegemite and a tub of cream cheese which we would devour at speed and then loll around feeling terrible, at which stage we would often go for the All-Bran in a bid to purge ourselves of the stodge. Either that or we would get a packet of gingernuts and a 2-litre tub of ice cream and devour that at speed as well. Of the four of us closest girlfriends, none had a healthy attitude towards food. I'm sure our families would be horrified if they knew the ruses we got up to involving eating, but honestly to us it seemed normal. And I'm sure parents today know little of what goes in or out of their daughters' mouths.

We loved taking laxatives. They just seemed like the perfect simple antidote to eating a lot — what joy! Often we would stuff ourselves with food (one friend's mother made a custard square that I would still cross two oceans to savour) and then OD on laxatives to feel thin again. It never occurred to us that this was in any way a damaging process that could wreak long-term havoc on our bowels, although we were all allegedly smart girls.

(Actually, I was one of only two girls in my class to not get accredited University Entrance, a fact that still riles me to this day. I got on a plane a year or so ago when I was editor of the *New Zealand Woman's Weekly* and there mistakenly sitting in my very seat was, coincidentally, the other unsuccessful accreditor. 'So what have you been doing?' I asked her of the intervening years. 'Well, I was a nun and now I'm a lesbian,' she replied. 'What are you doing?' Absolutely nothing of any interest in comparison, I thought.)

Our other speciality at school was stealing food, usually from Ann-Marie Delaney's schoolbag, and I'd like to take this opportunity to thank Mrs Delaney all these years later for her tireless contribution to my girth. Did you every wonder how Ann-Marie stayed so skinny but ate soooo many sandwiches? Interestingly, Ann-Marie is still very slim and very good-natured. We would wait for her to be engaged in a laughing fit or an intense conversation with someone else and then just help ourselves to the contents of her lunchbox. Sometimes, I would even take a bite or two and then put her sammies back as I was never that fond of raspberry jam no matter how desperate.

Our other source of food was, of course, the tuck shop. This could be raided in two ways: either with the help of the girls on the roster who manned it, or without. With just meant cajoling them outside the locked door until they let you in and turned a blind eye while you raided the ice cream freezer. Without meant jumping the counter and terrorising the good girls with your best Sister Eulalia skills while shoving cold pies up your jumper. That was my favourite, and to this day I fail to be repelled by cold pies.

As I said, my biggest mistake during these high school years was not to have a friend fatter than me, a fatal flaw I have tried to remedy ever since. I felt a lot fatter than I actually was, in stark contrast to more recent years where I suspect that I have felt thinner than I actually was. Would I have turned out differently if I had felt better about my body? Who knows? — but frankly I wouldn't miss those loaf of bread and tuck shop raid memories for the world.

The constant struggle I wage with my weight has made me the person I am today and, frankly, I'm not that bad. Sure, my corpulence has caused me my fair share of misery, but if it wasn't that, it probably would've been something else, most likely my hair. Thirty-five years down the track I now truly believe that your body is simply a suit you put on and that you should be more worried about what it's covering up than how it's covering it. The worst thing about being a porker is that as far as first impressions are concerned, it's right up there with ginger hair and buck teeth. But how many times have you struck up a conversation at a party with the spottiest, geekiest guy with the thickest spectacles out of sheer desperation and within minutes found yourself wetting your pants with laughter and swapping Fluffy Angel recipes? Not that often? OK, but how many friends have you dumped because they gained a few extra pounds? See, only one or two (although the correct answer is actually *none*). It really doesn't matter. It's just a suit. OK, so mine's a baggy, fat suit and I'd rather have a muscly, thin suit but what the heck! There's probably thousands of thin and muscly people out there who would just love to be round and cuddly. Unfortunately for them, all the real round, cuddly people would probably hate them for only pretending.

Incidentally, in a strange twist, I was kindly invited not to return to St Mary's after my sixth form year — and it was an invitation I graciously accepted.

- 4 -
Making a tit of yourself

In which bosoms are revealed to be much more worthwhile if they are proportionally bigger than the rest of you

LIKE WEIGHT, BOSOMS take up far too much of your average girls' worry quota. I mean, shouldn't we be saving some space for world peace or a cure for cancer or non-fat potato crisps or something? (By the way, for years I have been conducting my own intensive research into non-fat crisps and can reveal here for the first time that kettle frying is not the answer we are looking for.)

But back to boobs. It would definitely be easier on teenagers if their bosoms were all pretty much the same size and developed at pretty much the same time. Instead, some poor ten-year-olds start sprouting the most enormous ones you've ever seen while sixth formers at the same school are borrowing tuck shop money from everyone in sight to invest in the Elle McPherson push-up bra and other tricks you can do with mirrors.

My mum explained to me early on that I shouldn't expect too much on the front front because she had not been quick to develop in that area herself. The fact that I had outgrown her wedding outfit in the dress-up box by about the age of 11 made me wonder if we were in any way cut from the same cloth, so to speak, but I was in no hurry for bazookas anyway. In fact, she told me that sometimes they simply seemed to blossom overnight, so I'd usually give them a cursory glance first thing in the morning to see if the most recent overnight had been the one but I must have missed a day or two back in the 70s and all of a sudden, whoa, there they were, but I was in my late teens and not so sensitive by then anyway.

My first experience in the brassiere department scarred me mentally to the point where I only ventured back again recently, 20 years after the first nightmare.

Never one to discuss personal issues with anyone but my closest friends (um, unless you count the 900,000 readers of the *Woman's Weekly* and several hundred thousand Auckland radio listeners), at the age of 14 I mumbled something to Mum about my torso and we headed off to aforementioned undergarment department of James Smith's in Wellington.

The bra department was run by what looked like a heavily corseted bunch of elderly spinsters, possibly failed nuns, whose very eyes lit up at the sight of a virgin, unharnessed chest jiggling towards them beneath a face suffused with embarrassment.

Like vultures they swooped, the winner dragging me, I'm sure it was by the hair, into the closest changing room where my T-shirt was ripped off my back and my mounds fondled, I say *fondled*, with alacrity no less, by sharp and wrinkled talons.

Sadly for the raddled crone, I was simply not up to it. A few industrial-strength over-shoulder-boulder-holders were strapped around me, but I was bereft of the filling and after being clawed at for half an hour by the chief crone and a selection of her fellow ancient escapees from the local convent, I was released from my cubicle empty handed and bare chested. I think it's the only time I ever exited James Smith's at such speed that I overlooked the sweet department.

(Actually, James Smith's was home to a few groundbreaking moments in my teenage years. At about 17 I retired my horse, Gemmy, who had been given to me a few years earlier, and with the proceeds of the sale of my saddle, bought a 10-speed racing bike on the second floor of James Smith's which I carried down the escalator and rode jauntily through makeup and hosiery before being chased out by angry security men.

Perhaps it was their unsympathetic attitude towards my new purchase that egged me on about a year later to flirt with shoplifting in my old haunt. At the time it was very hip to own a pair of black faux leather (OK, vinyl) trousers and there was such a pair upstairs in the Expensive Department at James Smith's. Many times I went and looked at them, a couple of times I even tried them on, but the price tag made buying them altogether prohibitive. I think they were $175, which is a small fortune for plastic pants by today's standards, let alone those of the late 70s.

Such was my obsession with the plastic pants I hatched a plot by which I could become their owner without parting with any cash. I had a long camel coat that someone sensible had talked me into buying when I first started working, and because I had asked for a few extra inches in length to be added, it ended up brushing the floor. Wearing this coat and a long skirt underneath, I entered James Smith's with nothing but theft on my mind.

I took the trousers and a large selection of other garments into the cubicle with me and put on the vinyl pants. I rolled up the legs and stayed in there twiddling my thumbs for a bit and congratulating myself on my deviousness before returning all the other goods to the counter and walking out of the department. Down the escalator I strode, my new vinyl pants already creating a steamy friction between my thighs. Out through hosiery and makeup I strolled, casually retracing my steps of the previous year. I threw open the door to Cuba St, scanning behind me for the security men who'd gobbed off at me before. Nowhere to be seen. But, suddenly, what was this? I seemed to be uncommonly hot and sweaty underneath my stolen garb, oh, and the camel coat. My heart seemed to be pounding in my ears for some strange reason, when I knew it should be in my chest, although I never could recall what side it was on until I visualised the sacred heart of Jesus. Excuse me, did someone say *Jesus*? Jesus who brought us Moses who brought us the Ten Commandments one of which was Thou shalt not steal — *especially synthetic items of clothing that will probably only give you a rash?*

Cuba St buzzed and honked around me as I stood outside the doors of James Smith's, sweltering inside my stolen strides. I had indeed committed the perfect crime, but now I was just plain old scared of getting caught. What say I was hit by a bus and when the police were checking me for clean knickers as I'd always been promised they would, they discovered my fiendish handiwork? What a shrink. Wouldn't there be screams of laughter in court when the prosecutor yelled at me, 'So you put your reputation on the line for a garment totally devoid of man-made fibres?'

I turned around and re-entered the store, heading straight back upstairs for the Expensive Department from whence I had come. I gathered up a selection of clothes and took them into the cubicle where I removed the vinyl pants and returned them to the counter. My days as an international plastic pant smuggler were over.)

Back to bristols. As a result of being clawed at by those heinous harridans I went for 20 years without being properly fitted for a bra. As a teen, I discovered trainer bras which you could buy without being poked at by bony fingers, and from then on I've winged it on a selection of underwire lacey numbers which always look fabulous on a hanger.

Men assume that when women get together we talk about them and the size of their wedding tackle, but frankly the conversation is far more likely to turn first, to weight and then, often, bosoms.

As it turns out, bosoms are the hair of the torso, if you get my drift. If you have dark curls you want dead straight and blonde, and if you're ginger and straight you want mousy brown and frizzy (actually, not too many people want that). It's a bit simpler with bosoms. If you have poached eggs you dream of melons, and if you have melons you dream of poached eggs.

Either way, it's no easy matter getting just the right brassiere that will accentuate in the most flattering fashion whatever you have been given. My friend Kate has a set of hooters most women would die for. Not so big that she'd change her name to Chesty Morgan and wheel them around in a barrow calling herself the eighth and ninth wonders of the world or anything, but pretty good none the less.

Her problem was (and hands up who else has suffered from this) that while a brassiere would show her cleavage off to its full extent it would quite often give her a whole set of other bosoms on top of the ones she already had. And if she was totally unlucky she might find a third set around the back. And yes, true story, I do believe that if your brassiere is particularly ill-fitting you might also find a fourth set lurking under your armpits.

Which reminds me of a true story in which my own modest breasts played a lead role some years ago. When I lived in London I developed a mild phobia about travelling on the Underground, mostly because every time I tried it a completely mad person ended up sitting or standing right next to me — sometimes I even had one on either side! I later found out this is completely normal and got over it, but at the time I got around the getting from A to B business by riding a bike. The bike in itself had caused me a small amount of drama: once by being completely stolen from outside the Brixton police station, and then just one week later its replacement was mostly stolen from outside a cinema in Leicester Square, possibly the busiest part of London. When I went in to the movie it was a complete cycle locked through both front and back wheels to some iron railing. When I came out of the movie it was only the front and back wheels locked to the iron railing. Gone was the seat (most important), the pedals, the gears, the brakes and the handlebars. No one had seen a thing. It was the rebuilt version of this bike, with badly clashing fluorescent pink handlebars, that I was riding from work to my flat in North London when the strangest of things happened.

I was riding along a busy stretch of road not a mile from home, Walkman blaring in my ears, when I suddenly had the very odd sensation that my right breast was being squeezed. I looked down and, sure enough, it was! To my right was a nutter speeding along beside me on his racing bike, left hand outstretched, copping a right old feel. Well, imagine my surprise! 'Bugger off,' I yelled in horror, at which he hooted with laughter and whipped around in front of me and down a side street. Stunned by the proceedings of the last few seconds I got a wobble on and fell off into the traffic.

I picked myself up, dusted myself off and kept going, still shaking my head in disbelief at what had happened. I was just about to turn into my own street when I had the eerie sensation that my left breast was being squeezed. I looked down. It was — the bastard had come back for more! Can you believe the cheek?

Unfortunately, all I could think of to say was, 'Bugger off, I've already told you once,' which as a threat is hardly an incentive not to reoffend. Perhaps I could have said, 'Come round the back; I have an ill-fitting brassiere on, you may even find some more breasts back there!' but it didn't occur to me. Instead I left it at reiterating that he should bugger off which he did, hooting with laughter and blowing me kisses, do you mind, as I sprinted the last hundred yards to home where I got in the door and had to pinch myself (not on the breasts mind, they'd had enough for one day) to make sure it wasn't a dream.

It was such a peculiar thing to have happened that I became convinced it must be an English thing that no one had bothered to mention to me, like having to have a cheque guarantee card or queueing. At work the next day I casually mentioned, 'Oh by the way, I had my bosoms squeezed by a mad cyclist last night,' to see if my colleagues would merely roll their eyes and tsk tsk or actually show some surprise.

As it turns out, I am the only one I know of that this has ever happened to, so that, I suppose, is a small comfort — well, at least I'm not mad!

Anyway, back in New Zealand very recently, as several decades had passed since I had last been fitted for a brassiere, I decided perhaps I should take my life in my handfuls and pack them off for some special treatment. I had been wearing the same harnessing equipment for the past couple of years despite some alarming weight gains and losses, and it occurred to me that perhaps I was displaying more than one set.

I ventured into a new lingerie shop in Auckland and nervously fingered the Elle McPhersons before whispering to someone that I wanted my breasts measured.

Unfortunately, as it turns out he was just waiting for his girl-friend and ran from the store screaming, but I persisted despite my gross embarrassment. Finally, a mumsy type took pity on me and ushered me to the changing rooms which for a pleasant change were not communal. Imagine my horror when, after being measured in this confined space, I was broken the news that I had a set of 38C bosoms. Are you crazy? I wanted to shout at Mumsy. I'm flat-chested, that's what they told me last time. No wonder all those size 14 Elle McPherson jobs I'd been wearing for years were confusing those closest to me about what side of my body my bosoms were actually on! As it turns out, I thought, I'm built!

My joy and elation were short-lived when Mumsy returned to the cubicle on a quad bike towing a trailer load of the most industrial strength-looking harnessing equipment I've ever seen in my life. I realised then I was more 38 than C if you get my point. I mean the straps on some of these things were an inch wide. Nuns would be proud to get their digits on this hosiery. Nanna would love it for Christmas. But me? I'm used to sexy, even if it only fits half my body.

Half an hour later I was still in a lather of rejection and Mumsy was losing patience. Finally she said, 'You do know how to put a bra on, don't you?' Well, correct me if I'm wrong but you line your bosoms up with the bosom-shaped sockets and take it from there, if I'm not mistaken, although as it happens, I was. Apparently, in the 20 years since my emotional scarring at James Smith's a code of brassiere application has been developed by hosiery experts, and now the correct way to fill your brassiere as was demonstrated then and there for my benefit, is to bend over and shake your groove things then slip the equipment on while you're still letting it all hang out then stand up straight and, voila!

Not surprisingly after this revelation I was in a desperate rush to remove myself from the premises. Had everyone known about this dangly bosom thing for the last 20 years and never mentioned it to me? Finally I settled on a set of corsetry in which the straps were only half an inch thick but at least had a nice criss-crossy bit that went in the middle where my cleavage would no doubt be had I been dangling in the correct way for the past two decades.

On the way out of the shop, I used my special felt-tip to give the life-size cutout of Elle McPherson some realistic cellulite. That'll teach her.

- 5 -
Get a haircut and get a real job

**In which school is given the flick and the
pros and cons of diet pills are revealed**

TO QUANTIFY MY corpulence at this stage, I could buy jeans at the
shop, even if I did have to hook an upside-down coat hanger
through them to get the zip up (actually, that was quite normal
at the time), but could not wear skirts pleated or gathered at the
waist because of the generosity of my hips. In short, I was not too
deeply depressed about my form but I wasn't exactly jumping
around in a bikini either. Truly, if I could wear flares and look like
that now, I would not be writing this book.

I had talked my parents into letting me do my seventh form
year at Onslow College, the co-ed state school up the road where
I had been desperate to go for years because of rumours that pot
was smoked openly in the playground and cherry brandy drunk
during economics lessons. To a recent escapee from a Catholic
girls school this sounded like heaven but, cruelly, none of the
above turned out to be the case. Sadly, by the seventh form, the
pot smokers and cherry brandy drinkers had bunked off to
communes somewhere, leaving behind only the people who

actually wanted to sit their bursary exams and go on to university.

As I was not one of these I spent quite a lot of my school day elsewhere. Halfway through the year I pulled a legitimate sickie by coming down the stairs at home and telling my father over his poached eggs that I had to stay at home today as I had 'women's problems'. Like most men of his generation, the menstrual cycle was best not discussed over breakfast, although you think he would have found it slightly suspicious that I was using 'women's problems' as an excuse two or three times a week, every week. I guess he really, really, really didn't want to think about it that much.

When the family had cleared off that day, I set about finding myself a job, and rang up the *Dominion* newspaper to enquire about a position with them as an advertising representative. Unfortunately, not knowing what one was turned out to be a bit of a disadvantage and was picked up fairly early on in my conversation with the Personnel Manager, but still he asked me to come in and see him that afternoon, and after about an hour's chit-chat during which time he complimented me repeatedly on my height, he told me I could take my pick of three jobs. I bet that doesn't happen any more! I chose the job of Layout Girl in the ad department because the name had a nice ring to it.

I went home, broke the news to the family, started work about two weeks later and went flatting.

Our flat in Newtown cost the princely sum of $27 a week and I shared it with two girlfriends from school, Julie and Ronnie. Our lives revolved around eating and drinking, and we would often temper severe dieting bouts with waves of baking cakes and biscuits, often eating the mixture before it was cooked and washing the whole lot down with a cask of Fairhall River claret.

Ronnie even had a boyfriend who was vaguely into fitness, and if we were desperate we would gather all our change from around the house and make him run down to Kentucky Fried Chicken for a family pack, stopping at the pub on the way back for a bottle of gin.

Stuff It!

Our diets were legendary: if it didn't come from a Chinese health clinic or an Eastern European army camp we wouldn't countenance it. The weirder and less appetising the diet, the better. Of course, I think three days was the most we lasted, especially Julie and me. Ronnie could last much longer but in a strange and annoying twist actually had no extra weight to lose. Still, those saddlebags on her thighs formed her own personal hell. In retrospect, I should've rounded her up into a room with all the other thin girls who complained of being fat but weren't, and force fed them deep-fried Camembert with double chocolate chip ice cream until they burst out of their size 10s, but what can I say? She was a friend. I am happy to report that she went on to have two children in quick succession and finally got some serious flab of her own to talk about, which deeply warmed the cockles of our friendship and I am still dining out on that even though she has long since had her girlish figure back.

Yet again I made the huge mistake of not having a girlfriend fatter than me, so it's no surprise that I eventually discovered the joys of diet pills. If I had really thought about it, I would have known full well that diet pills were not a great idea. I mean, if it was that easy, why wasn't everyone knocking them back? Why were there any fat people? Why was the sky aubergine? Why did the measle have the cheese? (Oops, that's those other pills talking.)

But friendly Dr Feelgood in downtown Wellington could be talked into handing them out with the greatest of ease. All it took was a half-hearted explanation about how I was going to do PE training at Otago (yeah, right, after the eighty-eighth time, Doc, ain't you getting a little suspicious?) and there was the prescription in the usual illegible handwriting being slid across the desk. The whole process of obtaining said prescription took less than three minutes. I guess he weighed me, but I probably never looked. Then down to the chemist and $35 later I was the proud owner of a month's supply of tenuate dospan — the antidote to fine dining.

Stuff It!

So started a six-month period of starvation which I have to say was most effective in its results. Every morning I would jump up and pop a diet pill then race off to work where I would drink copious amounts of coffee and smoke a zillion cigarettes. Sometimes I got a headache but then I took disprin. Usually I wouldn't eat anything all day but have a small meal at night, and at one stage I was only eating three sesame crackers with pâté a day.

I must confess the thrill of extra-fast weight loss is absolutely addictive. Of course, it's a while since I experienced it firsthand and I am probably immune to diet pills now, but back then, oh the power, the joy of growing smaller. Every day your trousers are looser. Every week you can tighten your belt an extra notch. Each time you go shopping for clothes you can slip on something more close-fitting. It's better than eating (OK, that *is* the diet pills talking).

Now, I thought such rapid weight loss was perfectly normal — well, given that I wasn't eating anything, how could it be otherwise? — but my colleagues at work obviously didn't agree, and the fact I was disappearing before their very eyes did not seem to please them as much as it pleased me. One day they approached me at morning tea-time with a pottle of yoghurt and tried to make me eat it. I was in an absolute panic — why were they plotting against me? — and grabbed one of them, a friend of mine, aside, and begged her to take the yoghurt away without forcing it on me.

I seriously thought they were all stark, raving, loonies from some strange alien planet where eating yoghurt sucked the life right out of you and possibly even turned you into one of them, which meant spending the rest of your life in a zip-up silver all-in-one suit which frankly, girlfriend, never did a thing for nobody. I did not think my behaviour was at all bizarre.

It's one of the great, tragic memories of my life that I remember standing on the scales (well, of course you have scales if you're losing weight, silly! — it's when you're gaining weight they go out the window) at that stage in my life cursing them because I weighed 9 st 2 lb. I was 5′ 10″, 19 years of age, had cheekbones like triangles and a chin that could open canned goods, and I was wild about those two and a bit measly pounds that were keeping me from weighing 8 st something.

I have to say, it is an interesting phenomenon that I can still stand on scales and curse them for not letting me weigh 9 stone, although it is 2 stone (or 4 or 6) that is keeping me away, not 2 (or 4 or 6) pounds. The point is, the amount of extra weight isn't proportional to how bad you feel about it, so, in other words, whether you're a little bit overweight or a lot, you're often the same amount of shitty and where, for God's sake, is the sense in that?

Yes, yes, yes, I said I can still stand on scales — I didn't say I actually did. Yeez, I wish I'd never mentioned anything about the scales now.

I never did get down to 9 stone, as it happens. I have an inherent love of food that will always stop me from being anorexic, and without diet pills I could not have forgone it for so long. Also, I hadn't had a crap in so long that I felt like the Christmas turkey, know what I'm saying? Because I ate so little, laxatives were useless, and an old but faithful trick of eating a box of liquorice and washing it down with red wine now only made me sick and failed to relieve my tortured bowels. It was time for common sense to step in.

I said, it was time for common sense to step in.

Oh, yes, there it was. It had been sitting in an abandoned chocolate box under my bed gathering slut's wool for six months while I starved myself, but in the nick of time, it came to my rescue and saved me from being a size eight. I came off the diet pills. Without them, I was a different person. Man, those tenuate dospan make you cranky! Of course, I was a hungry person, but at least I smiled before I ate.

Around this time I had my hair dyed in black and white checks. Some people in the alternative scene at the time may have thought this was pretty interesting but if they did, I never met them, and personally I had my doubts as, actually, it was something of a mistake. No, I mean a genuine mistake. I was having my hair 'trimmed' at a salon across the road from work and I guess the huge puffs of strong, rope-smelling smoke billowing out of the morning tea cubicle should have alerted me to the fact that it was quite a creative morning at Furballs or whatever it was called.

Anyhow, when the hairdresser came out red-eyed and asked me what my favourite shape was, I didn't know I was going to end up with it on the back of my head, so I told him it was black and white checks, as I was going through a strict monochrome phase at the time. Just as well I never said purple banana-shaped phalluses, I guess! Two hours later I had a darn checkerboard peroxided on the back of my head. There weren't too many of Furballs' Fabulous Checkerboard Heads in Wellington in 1981, so my coif ended up on the front page of the evening newspaper; an event that prompted my entire family to stop speaking to me for a month and my brother to put an ad in the paper saying he was not related to me.

So blood is thicker than water but not as thick as peroxide, eh? Oh, but I'm not bitter. No. No way. Still, come the revolution they'll all have checkerboards on their heads and *I'll* have purple banana-shaped phalluses on mine, and so will begin my evil plan for world domination. Ha ha ha ha (maniacal laugh).

Now, where was I? Oh yes. Without the diet pills I was eating my way up to a normal weight, and so absconded on holiday to Nelson where a friend and I planned to ride a horse and cart around the area for a couple of weeks. We hitchhiked down to Appleby, me wearing a hat so as not to frighten the kiddies, and picked up our Clydesdale, Bonita, and our red and blue covered buggy. I felt just like Clint Eastwood in *Paint Your Wagon* — only with a checkerboard hairdo and bosoms.

Our idyllic back-to-nature trip didn't take long to go awry, however. For a start, Bonita did not seem to take kindly to our instructions of 'giddyup' and 'whoa', and in fact seemed totally confused about the difference. As a result, it was a pretty hit and miss affair whether we stopped or started and the decision was never really ours. But when we did get going we attracted quite a bit of attention. It's not often down in those parts, or any other parts for that matter, that you would hear the clitter clatter of a horse and wagon, and come outside your farmhouse to see two punks and a Clydesdale pulling a red and blue wagon doing the equine equivalent of a bunny-hop up the road. Our first day on the road we clattered into Brightwater, stopping in a kind and considerate way to be admired and talked to by the locals.

Our first port of call, and our first mistake as it turns out, was at the Brightwater Pub for a crate of Steinlager. Them loaded up, we clattered even more noisily into a public park which was down a track off the main road. We unhitched the horse to let it graze on the lush-looking grass, and set about having a refreshing ale to take the edge off our thirst on such a beautiful, hot, summer's day. Four Steinlagers later we were both snoring our heads off in the sweltering heat and awoke with a start about an hour later.

The horse, of course, was gone.

Deeply hysterical and with heads aching from too much beer, we scoured the neighbouring undergrowth and woods for the missing Clydesdale. I mean, how can you lose a Clydesdale?

Finally, I ran down the track to the main road, and looking back in the direction from whence we came, thought I could make out a Clydesdale-like figure holding up traffic on a one-way bridge in the distance.

I took to my scrapers with a speed that has never been rivalled before or since. Embarrassingly, all the families who had come out to admire us as we drove into town, came out again for a good laugh as I chased after that bitch Bonita.

When I finally reached the bridge, exhausted, someone had had the brains to get out and catch her. Mumbling and wheezing my thanks, I snatched her from him and took her behind the first tree I came to, where I gave her a good kick in the guts and she bit me on the bum. It seemed only fair.

- 6 -
Diet? Kill it!

In which every half-baked army, mental institute or minor food group has a diet named after it

THE STUPIDEST THING about losing weight is that it is actually very simple. All you have to do is eat less and exercise more. What could be simpler? Then why, I hear you ask, haven't you just done it? Well, obviously if I knew the answer to that I wouldn't be sitting here guiltily writing this book knowing that I have squeezed in an extra breakfast today. I would be shopping on Rodeo Drive with the proceeds of the book I wrote 20 years ago revealing the easy way of eating less and exercising more.

'You're either fat or you're hungry,' a fellow weight-watcher pointed out to me recently. 'Just pick which one you can stand the most and get used to it.'

'Make hunger your friend,' was the advice from another source, who I am assuming was of Red Indian extraction.

But perhaps the trouble here is that the eat less/exercise more scenario is just too easy for us to contemplate. I mean nobody goes to the appliance store and buys the VCR with only one button, do they? No, you want the one with all the whistles and bells and functions you'll never even know about let alone understand, and as for using them — hah! Plus you want an instruction manual that makes *War and Peace* look like junk mail. That's value for money, that is.

So, too, I think it is with diets.

Why just eat less and run about more when there are lots of other magical tricks you can use that will cost you heaps of money and probably not even work into the bargain?

After all, don't we have to keep Jenny Craig in the style to which she has become accustomed, according to the latest *Under the Loggia With Jenny* spread in some glossy magazine or other? There are millions around the world whose livelihoods rely on us picking an expensive and complicated way to eat less and lose more. It would be cruel to deny them their living just because the answer lies in keeping less food in your fridge and walking around the block every now and then.

The Mayo Clinic Diet was one of the first I can remember attempting semi-seriously. When my girlfriends and I attempted it together, we actually thought the Mayo bit referred to mayonnaise — or, more likely, the lack of it. Well — we were hungry! Imagine our surprise when we discovered that the Mayo in the diet was not named after a high cholesterol salad dressing but a family of medical practitioners who started up their own clinic in Minnesota in 1903. Whatever its origins, of all the diets I have ever been on I think this one made me the hungriest. The first day you ate five hard-boiled eggs, nothing else. The second day it was tomatoes and dry toast. The third day more eggs and spinach. The fourth day lamb and eggs and tomatoes, and the fifth day — well, I never made it to the fifth day so I don't know. All I do know is that the only way to succeed on this diet is to be in a coma for the whole time. Have you ever tried to eat five hard-boiled eggs in one day? I practically still have a lump in my chest where those eggs were.

I tried this diet several times and never lost a pound. *Quelle surprise!* But other people (sure, none that I knew, but they were out there) could go on it for two weeks and lose half a stone, which at the time seemed a lot of weight to not have any more. Nowadays it's lunch, but there you have it.

The Israeli Army Diet was another one doing the rounds in the early 80s. Again, at the time we were a bit confused about this diet, thinking it was the Swiss Army Diet named after the pocket-knife popularised many years later by fictional TV action man McGyver, a personal favourite of mine, incidentally, but entirely irrelevant to a book examining the lighter side of dieting which is why I've slipped him in here but it's a oncer.

This diet was just as much of a killer as the brainchild of the pork-busting practitioners from Minnesota, starting off with two days of eating apples, followed by two days of eating cheese, followed by two days of eating chicken. Excuse me? Two days of eating cheese? That's OK if the Israelis wanted the enemy to win the war, but it was shit-useless in the battle of the bulge, let me tell you. Strangely, I never got past day five on this one either, and again never lost a pound. I have a strange fixation with chicken, though, which I can trace back to the Whatever Army It Was Diet, which is mildly interesting but nonetheless leaves me with a strange fixation with chicken.

A weight-loss programme of my own invention was the Incredible Raspberry Diet. This involved going down to Nelson to pick raspberries for the summer in a scheme the Labour Department assured us was a sure-fire winner on the savings front. Myself and three girlfriends were further lured southward by the promise of many local lads queueing up on a Friday night at the gates of the raspberry farm to which we had been assigned.

When we got there, however, it soon became clear to us that the local lad lure was simply a ruse to get us down to Mrs Crank's farm where we were to be used as slave labour. Four of us were housed in a shack no bigger than a broom cupboard, with the only toilet a long-drop several hundred metres away. Considering I thought a long-drop was a kind of earring this ablution facility came as something of a shock to me, and I havn't been able to go anywhere where there are not proper toilets ever since, and I am including major continents here.

We were woken at 7 a.m. to be out in the raspberry patch or whatever it's called at eight. There you were given a metal pot that was strapped around your belly; you filled the pot with raspberries and emptied it into a bin at the end of your row. When the bin was filled, it was weighed at the shed and its weight recorded next to your name, forming the basis on which you were paid. I was not a bad picker. But I ate a lot of raspberries. I made $13.87 in one week.

Come the second Friday night in Mrs Crank's hell-hole there was again a yawning absence of local lads queueing up at the gates. We packed our bags and were chased down the driveway by Mrs Crank, who farewelled us with curses and taunts of 'G-strings, girls — you're not worth a tin of fish, anyway.'

That diet would probably have been more successful had I not spent my raspberry-picking riches subsidising my raspberry intake with Cornish pasties from the Ruby Bay dairy. Again, though, it has to be said, my weight problem at that stage was far more in my mind than on my bones, and so diets simply didn't take the way they have in more recent years.

OK, so who remembers the Bread Diet? Now there was a dumb idea if ever I tried one. Eat as much bread as you can stuff down one day, then normal food the next. The catch was that the bread couldn't have anything on it, and especially not butter, which as we all know is usually the only reason why you bother with bread in the first place. I still can't look at a Molenberg roll without belching repeatedly and rushing for the Eno's. Now I do know people (OK, person, one person) who had great results with this diet, but I had too much difficulty getting through the bread-only days, and on the days that I could do it, I made up for it the next day by eating twice my normal amount of food — which was quite a lot. Also, by this stage, my bones had caught up with my mind regarding my weight problem. Tragically, my poor old brain seemed sadly confused by the Bread Diet, and didn't seem to want to budge any of my extra fatty deposits.

A few years later the Micro-Diet seemed an answer to my prayers, because not only did it come in packets, but it also cost loads of money which I assumed guaranteed its success. Once a week I would sneak over to a salesperson's private residence in Wellington and stock up on powders, soups and special bars that tasted like dried-up chipboard. The plan with this diet was to substitute powdered drinks for whole meals; this worked a treat as long as you didn't then get hungry and have the meals anyway. The drinks were yummy. Hey, even the chipboard tasted OK if you were starving. But something was still missing. I suppose it was food.

I watched a hilarious episode of 'Oprah Winfrey' once when she was interviewing expanding soul singer Luther Van Dross. Oprah and Luther were both chunky at the time as they had each virtually doubled their body weights, having previously lost themselves on liquid diets. A montage of their appearances together over the years was most confusing. First a fat Oprah talks to a fat Luther. Then fat Oprah talks to thin Luther. Then thin Oprah talks to thin Luther. Then thin Oprah talks to fat Luther. Then fat Oprah talks to fat Luther again.

Oprah's thin again now and has to stay that way because she's written a book on how to do it (gulp and read chapters 18, 19 and 21), but Luther is still up and down like a bride's nightie and apparently very touchy on the subject should you bump into him at your next Weightwatcher's meeting.

I wonder if Luther ever tried the Grapefruit Diet? This was another one that did the rounds of the ill-informed. I can remember doing it with my flatmates once; we ate grapefruit before every meal so that the juice could 'break down the fat' and limit the effects of our indulgence. However, a rumour then swept through the flat that we had got the wrong end of the stick, and so we had a crack at eating grapefruit *after* every meal so that the acids could then go to work on what we had already eaten.

I swear, if we had put the same amount of effort into cooking decent food as we had into dreaming up crackpot diets, we'd probably, um, still be experimenting with crackpot diets.

Now, Pritikin! There was another one. Why should we stick at it when even Pritikin himself couldn't bear to be on it another day and topped himself?

The Scarsdale Diet is not one I tried myself, but my father used to go on it with fairly reliable results. He'd stick to it for two weeks and generally lose half a stone, which is the way diets are supposed to go. But I didn't want to lose my weight on an old man's diet — it was bad enough that my Dad and I both liked Billy Joel's *The Stranger* album — so I rudely ignored it.

Rosemary Conley's Hip and Thigh Diet is not one on which I have had a great amount of success myself, but it is probably the closest to what I eat now. Her basic rule is cut out the fat and keep up the exercise, but there is something in my brain (which I'm sure weighs more than the average one owing to there being lots of interesting diet information stored in it, thus pushing me up the weight-for-height chart) that stops me from being able to go on a diet if it is called a diet.

Myself and my husband did try the Hip and Thigh Diet for a few months when we were living in London, and it was my first experience of the it's-my-diet-so-how-come-he's-losing-all-the-weight syndrome. Mark had only agreed to go on the pesky thing to give me a bit of support. Being of similar build, we both ate exactly the same amount of the same things, and while I had a more sedentary job, I was countering this by exercising at the gym three or four times a week. The weight just dropped off him. It stuck to me like glue. This is possibly about the most annoying thing that can happen to a couple.

In the end, the poor wretch had to sneak off to secret rendezvous with Wimpy bars and McDonald's all over London outside of meal times to avoid losing weight himself while appearing to support me in my endeavours, otherwise I would have been cranky.

It's a measure he still takes to this day. I can stand a lot of things, but a man with a bottom smaller than mine, never — and this he knows.

Now that I'm trying not to try to be like Elle McPherson — no matter how unsuccessful I was in the first place — I laugh at most diets I see advertised and very rarely pursue them.

Having said that, though, it takes quite a lot of training to get out of the habit of truly, deep-down believing that there is a magical answer to your weight problem that will probably come in a box and cost lots of money.

I know for a fact that I won't go on another diet if it's called a diet, or even if it isn't called a diet but is something else simply masquerading as a diet. But sitting in my office the other day I heard an ad on the radio. 'Sick of being overweight? Tired of not fitting into those jeans? Disillusioned with spending dollar after dollar on products that never work? Fed up with exercise? Then you need to call us on 0800 LARD ARSE.' I eyeballed the phone, but my hands stayed sitting under my bum (and my husband tells me it's quite hard to get out from this position).

Make hunger your friend, I told myself. Eat less and exercise more. Be fat or hungry. Get used to it. The desire to pay anyone any money to tell me any of these things passed once I remembered that I already knew them for myself. My dieting days are over.

I must say, though, I cacked myself over one recent advertising claim that proved there are crackpot ideas out there that are even more stupid than diets. In this ad, a has-been 'celebrity' revealed she had lost three pounds (exclamation mark, exclamation mark) by using a special seaweed soap. Three pounds? Excuse me, that's one good crap! You could probably lose more weight eating seaweed soap. Exclamation mark. Exclamation mark.

- 7 -

My name is Sarah-Kate and I am a fat chick

In which large groups of overweight people get together and put ideas into each others' heads that weren't there before and which mean stopping at the bakery on the way home

THE FIRST TIME I ever went to Weightwatchers I was wearing a St Mary's school uniform, and I wasn't on my way to an Association of Chief Executives cocktail party, either. I was about 16 and crippled with self-consciousness about my chubbiness. I'd gone with a friend who was quite a bit thinner than me but had more cellulite, which made us kind of even.

I liked the fact that at Weightwatchers they gave you a book with everything that you could eat written down on a day by day basis — that seemed pretty organised. And I liked the fact that you got a sticker like an old-fashioned tram ticket to put in your Weightwatchers book every week you turned up. I did not like the fact that you were weighed and no matter how much you rocked back on your heels, the scales told no lies, plus the person in the queue behind you could get a squiz at the awful truth and I knew that for a fact because I had eyeballed the scales myself when the person in front of me jumped on them.

Neither did I like the fact that the meetings themselves bordered on audience participation, and I am the sort of person who will request a seat in the middle of Aisle X behind the pillar at a Topp Twins concert just to avoid even the fear of being dragged on to the stage and made a laughing stock. In this vein, Weightwatchees were invited to 'share' their loss or gain, and then a group discussion would start up.

Despite these drawbacks, I embraced the Weightwatchers philosophy for about the first two weeks — and guess what? I lost about half a stone and then put it straight back on the moment I dropped out.

The next time I went to Weightwatchers I was about ten years older and dragged along another 'virgin' friend who I took into the loos on the way up to the meeting and instructed on the ritual of removing all loose change, belts, earrings and preferably the contents of one's bowels before fronting up for the weigh-in. The lecturer at this group was a particular lemon who seemed to know very little about anything except for the fact that she had lost 12 stone or some other astounding amount by attending Weightwatchers herself and was rewarded by being appointed the Akela for fresh blood such as ourselves.

As an example of her lack of helpfulness, when my friend asked why you were encouraged to drink water instead of Diet Pepsi, tea or coffee while you were trying to lose weight, the lecturer said she couldn't remember. After the weigh-in, the caring and sharing session, and the ensuing group discussion, she whisked off to use the phone and came back crowing, 'Now I remember, now I remember. It's because you wouldn't use Diet Pepsi or tea or coffee to rinse out the kitchen sink now, would you?' Not surprisingly, we felt her credibility slipping away from us and were forced to go immediately to the excellent fish and chip shop in Molesworth St to mull over her wisdom.

I did lose weight on that occasion as I was discovering jazz-ergetics at the same time but, guess what? It came back again.

The next time I tried the watching style of weight-loss I was living in London and used to sneak away from work at lunch times to go to a group meeting in Oxford St, often stopping to buy a pair of ill-fitting but very reasonably priced shoes on the way. To my horror, there were none of the huge porkers I had come to expect at other Weightwatchers meetings that always made me feel like the 'slip of a girl' I so desired to be. In fact, I seemed to be one of those porkers, so help me God!

By the way, if you think I am being secretive about how much I actually weighed during these times, I am not. As you may have gathered, I have a pathological fear of numbers when it comes to their representation of my size, and I have obviously blocked all numerals from my mind. The only gauge I can give you is that at my lightest, at 17, I weighed about 58 kilos, and at my heaviest, at 33, I weighed about 110 — but those are Australian kilos so they might not count. All the other times, including now, I have been in between, but let's be honest, I'm not going to be 58 kilos again until I'm dead or seriously depleted of limbs by way of a nasty knitting accident.

The other thing I found contemptible about the English Weightwatchers was that when you emptied your pockets and jumped on the scales, your weight was shouted, nay, trumpeted, across the room by a big blonde strumpet with a Cockney accent, in a way that left the words ringing in my ears for, oh, about six years. What a disaster. I persevered for as long as I could, but it was yet another failure. Perhaps I should have taken heed of the first two failed attempts.

I tried Weightwatchers once more when I moved to Auckland in the mid 90s, but by this stage I was becoming a Weight-watching rebel and everything the lecturer said made me want to roll my eyes and go tsk tsk tsk with my tongue, and it was altogether too much like being back in 6A.

I know that Weightwatchers has worked very well for some people, including the Duchess of York, Sarah Ferguson, who is now the million-dollar spokesperson for the group's American arm, although she is delightfully vague on exactly which programme it was that led to her shedding of kilos. However, I also know that for other people it is just a short-term remedy that never really confronts the issues of why they eat too much and how they can knock that on the head for good.

Do you know what I think the problem is? They are always blathering on about food! Yes, that's where they go wrong. It's all food this, eat that, cook this, nibble on the next thing. Honestly, quite often those meetings will put ideas into your head about food you hadn't even realised was on the planet. I remember listening to one poor woman telling the story of her struggle with the supply of peanut slabs she kept for her kids; this chocolate seemed to appear to her in visions at least 20 times a day, whispering, 'eat me, eat me, remember — brown food doesn't have calories'. Well, do you think I could get that confectionery out of my mind? Not on your thigh — I mean, life. I couldn't rest until I went out and had a peanut slab for myself, and I don't even really like chocolate. How clever is that? Do you know, the only time I have ever eaten Kentucky Fried Chicken is on my way home from a Weightwatchers meeting. True story.

The constant chat at Weightwatchers about what to eat and when to eat it is enough to drive anybody mad, especially anybody on a diet. Who wants to be constantly planning and chopping and avoiding and dicing and shopping and weighing when all you want to do is eat less and get on with things? I now believe that the only way to take weight off for good is to find a system that fits into the life you are already leading and takes your mind off eating — and no, it doesn't involve amphetamines.

The other thing all Weightwatchers meetings seem to have in

common (apart from the fact that nobody trusts the maximum signs in the elevators) is the hideousness of the rooms in which they are held. Perhaps those of you with lifetime memberships and hipbones will be shaking your heads angrily and polishing your badges, but honestly, I've yet to attend a meeting that hasn't been held in the equivalent of the Eketahuna Crumbly Old Man's Dusty Balls Clubhouse, complete with toilets that are reluctant to flush and mirrors that make you look ten times bigger than you actually are. OK, so maybe you actually are that big, but that's no excuse for running out of lav paper.

Jenny Craig is another weight-loss organisation in which I proved to be a total failure. I was propelled there only because I had six months to halve my bulk before I got married, and a friend had achieved remarkable results with Jenny Craig's nuke-it or puke-it powdered, tinned and otherwise packaged fodder. I would hazard a guess that 50 per cent of the devotees to Jenny's cuisine are young women with wedding bells ringing in their ears and spare tyres flailing around their middles.

My first visit entailed having a very unflattering fat photo taken, being weighed, being privately counselled and attending a group session. The private counselling wasn't too bad because I promptly pointed out to my counsellor that I wasn't really there for the chit-chat but was a serial weight gainer and loser, and needed to shift some pounds in order to avoid looking like a three-tiered cream cake on my wedding day. End of story. This went down pretty well.

The group session — now there was another story. Somewhere along the line Jenny must have gotten being 'fat' confused with being 'stupid', because that's how we devotees were treated.

'Now, when we are overweight we have no self-esteem,' we were told. 'When we go to parties we stand at the back feeling out of place and uncomfortable, don't we?'

My blood was boiling as I fought the urge to chip in that hadn't she ever heard of fat and jolly? I mean, I know that thin and jolly is better, but hey, enough of the bring-down talk already. With my eyes rolling around in my head and the tsk tsk tsks welling up in my throat, I excused myself from the depression chamber and went to pick up the assorted tins and sachets that would feed me for the next week.

A lot of the Jenny Craig food made me retch the minute I opened it, and the fact that some things came in tins and looked just like jellimeat didn't exactly help, but a couple of the pasta dishes I really took to. OK, so sometimes I had to cook two at once (just can't get enough of that Pasta Alfredo) just to feel even half-full, but by the time our nuptials rolled around I was 10 kilos lighter than when I walked in the door at Jenny Craig that first day.

I was very quick to lose weight off my fingers on Jenny Craig. Maybe it was a retention thing. Anyway, one day when it was particularly cold, my engagement ring became very loose and slippery on my ring finger, so I put it on my middle finger. The ring itself was something of a sore point because I had never been a ring-wearing person before and felt slightly uncomfortable about changing sides. To go with my yam-like toes, the joke of my friends and family, I have quite sausagey fingers. (I'm sure it's no coincidence that so many of my body parts resemble food.) Wearing a ring did nothing for the meat-like consistency of my hands, but it did prove to girls much thinner and prettier than me that I had nabbed me a fiancé. There was one humiliating experience, though, in the bowels of Broadcasting House, where I bumped into two other fiancées and the old 'I'll show you mine if you show me yours' brawl erupted. Once I could see again after being blinded by the glint of the fluorescent lights hitting their huge rocks, we set about trying to find my diamond, but when their eyes met sympathetically over my tiddly little twinkle I put my sausages back in my pocket and took off in a huff.

The ring went on to cause me some pain the day after it swapped digits because the thing that had gone away to make my ring finger too skinny came back, only now my ring was on my not-skinny-either middle finger, and would not come off. Embarrassingly enough, I eventually had to go home from work early because my finger had swelled up to the size of a salami, and despite everybody's hints on how to get rid of the blasted thing it was going nowhere and my typing was becoming full of dddddddds and ffffffffffs. At home, I soaked the offending finger in a bowl of ice and dishwashing liquid for half an hour, and then pulled the ring off so viciously it flew across the room and landed in my flatmate's cactus plant which pricked me as I fished it out. Honestly, it's a miracle the wedding ever went ahead.

But it did and my wedding day is still the best day of my life. I felt a million dollars minus those 10 Jenny Craig kilos. Course, by the time the honeymoon was over, the honeymoon was over. Those darn kilos were back and not budging — but at least I had me a husband and could let myself go.

I know a few people who still use Jenny Craig as a get-thin-quick scheme when they want to shed extra kilos in a hurry for special occasions, but there's not too many long-term success stories among them. In fact, none that I know of.

My weight-watching and Jenny Craig days are well and truly behind me now. I firmly believe that for me, being amongst other overweight people on a regular basis is more of an encouragement to remain that way than an enticement to change.

Now put me in a room full of Pamela Andersons once a week and I'm sure I'd change my tune, *tout de suite*, and get the number of the hottest liposuction guy in town. I know that seems sad and not at all politically correct, but if you are not motivated by jealousy of women thinner than you then you're probably a stick figure to begin with and should get out of this book immediately because we hate skinny minnies like you! I suppose you can eat and eat and eat all you want and never put on a pound. Well, go on then — dial a pizza!

If every single woman in the world weighed 110 kilos, would you seriously starve yourself down to 58? I don't think so.

- 8 -
Move those buns, Rita!

If it makes you hot and sweaty and leaves you wishing you were dead, it's probably exercise

FOR ME, THE JOY of exercise will never be outdone by the joy of sitting at home on the sofa watching crappy American TV.

I am constantly waging an internal struggle between exercising and staying at home, and sometimes I do get up off my butt, but moving around quickly (unless it's a lolly scramble) will never come naturally, I know this for a fact.

For example, I should be at the gym right now, but I am not. In fact, I so desperately want to be any place other than there that I have just spent two hours cleaning out the kitchen cupboards in a bid to deliberately run out of time.

In a strange twist, I will wake up tomorrow and think of a whole new bunch of ways to deliberately run out of time, which in itself can be quite exhausting but at least the chores get done, yet it will not occur to me to a) actually go to the gym or b) for God's sake shut up and stop whining.

Ever since I can remember I have not liked moving around very quickly or, in fact, much at all. I was made to go to modern ballet as a littlie because my feet did peculiar things that made wearing shoes difficult. Sadly, my feet did even more peculiar things during ballet classes, and they weren't the peculiar things being asked of them, either.

My major disappointment with this form of exercise was that being 'modern' there were no tutus, and instead I had a plain pink dress that was salvaged credibility-wise only by having a pair of matching knickers.

The teacher was a sort of deranged escapee from the Anna Pavlova Home for the Dangerously Co-ordinated, and for some reason I have always remembered her as Miss Sebastian Cabot, although that is actually the name of the man who played the housekeeper on that crappy American TV show with the single father whose kids were called Buffy and Jodie. Know the one?

Miss Sebastian Cabot's interpretation of modern ballet for five-year-olds meant requiring them to run around and act like an autumn leaf falling from a tree. Now I had a pretty active imagination at this stage, but no matter how hard I tried I always felt much more like the leaf that would stay firmly attached to the branch, thank you very much. Anyway, one day during the class Miss S.C. asked me to walk forty blocks to get her an Eskimo Pie. When I got back, I realised all the other autumn leaves had been performing for their parents during my absence. I was the equivalent of the only kid in the choir asked to just mouth the words. Actually, I was the only kid in the choir asked to just mouth the words, too. And now, my career as a ballerina was over as well. What was I going to get for Christmas — a car accident?

Still, as we sports enthusiasts like to say, never mind.

Softball and gymnastics were also out because of big eggs on my head. In fact, it's a wonder I can remember a thing given the number of times I've been whacked on the scone. Just as well I'm so good at making things up, what! As a five-year-old I was hit on the head with a baseball bat and rendered confused for quite some time — in fact, I may have already mentioned this, I just can't remember. What I was doing wandering around the batting area at the time no one could ever quite work out, so I think it only fair to say that I was not a natural on the diamond in the first place.

My flirtation with gymnastics happened outside the Moana Pools (yes, them again) when, like other girls obviously shorter than me, I was attempting to swing around the bars put up to lean your bike against. Had I been further up the mathematics trail I would have worked out the distance between the bar and the ground was far less than the distance between my head and the hips from which I was swinging. As it was, I worked it out the moment my forehead cracked against the concrete, but I instantly forgot it again. Strangely, as a result of that knock I did remember where I left the chocolate buttons I had hidden from my sister when I was four.

No wonder then, that after disasters of these proportions I was much more inclined to be slumped on a beanbag somewhere than enjoying physical activity. By my teenage years, when I recognised that exercise could perhaps help release me from the torture of my chubby body, I had a whole other problem to worry about. *What am I going to wear?* In the 70s, there didn't seem to be anything a self-conscious, slightly overweight teenager could wear to flatter the curves.

As I've said, often it was rompers, which as we have discussed, are especially designed to explode the hips in a round-the-world-air-ballooning sort of a way. Netball skirts were so short that they couldn't be countenanced if you were the least bit worried about your wobbly thighs. And as for Speedos, well, we all know there's no hiding a thing when you are in your togs — swimming was out of the question, too.

It seems ridiculous now to think that fear of looking flabby was responsible for avoiding so many different forms of exercise, but I bet I'm not the only one who thought that way then, and I bet there are teenage girls out there thinking like that now, although

Stuff It!

I have to say that cycling shorts are something of a revolution.

I tried playing squash with my father once, but after 55 attempts to hit that little ball with that little racquet — all unsuccessful — we gave up. Tennis I liked the idea of, but the same lack of hand-eye co-ordination meant you wouldn't want me on your team, sort of thing. Hockey we never played at our school, thank goodness, as with my history of getting beaten around the head with sporting implements it could have been the difference between passing UE or not. (Did I pass it or not? Shoot, I just can't remember. What day is it today, anyway?) Running I have tried three times in my life and each time I have vomited. But horse-riding, now there's a different story!

Riding is the only form of exercise at which I am not completely useless, and that is obviously because the horse does most of the work.

When I was twelve, I asked for a rusty, red, Raleigh 20 bike for Christmas. Dad worked in finance and just about always had a mate who could get him a cheap deal on whatever it is you wanted Santa to provide. Unfortunately, the mate didn't always work to the elves' timetable, and in this case it was nearly my birthday in May before I realised that the rusty, red, Raleigh 20 was not a happening thing. At this stage I was told I could have a blue Loline bike or choose something else. A Loline? Were they mad? What a shrink! No thanks. I'll have a pony instead. I never could understand what made my parents laugh so much that day. I had been reading more *Jill Has Two Ponies* and *Bunty's Dream Jumper* than was good for me, and had been lulled into the hope that gypsies would provide me with a moth-eaten old piebald won in a game of gin rummy, who with my love and attention and loads of horse nuts would eventually win all the ribbons at the gymkhana.

When it was pointed out to me that gypsies were a bit thin on the ground in Khandallah, Wellington, I cut a different deal with the olds. Horse-riding lessons on a Saturday morning. Every week

I'd pull my jodhpurs on and Dad would take me out to Ohariu Valley to get yelled out by some mean old lady for an hour, then bring me home, deliriously happy.

I'm sure my parents thought this was just a phase I was going through, but after two years of lessons I was still keen as mustard and was eventually offered a horse of my own by a family who had outgrown theirs, but didn't want to sell her.

Gemmy was 23-years-old and legend had it she had been ousted from the Wairarapa Hunt Club for overtaking the huntsmen and trampling on the hounds. She was big and solid and chestnut and had a mouth of iron. She stopped only when she wanted to and don't you forget it. I borrowed all the gear I needed to ride with and begged Mum and Dad to pay the grazing fee. Never a graceful equestrian, as you can probably imagine, I became very good at never falling off. I know it's not much in terms of sporting achievements but, hey, it's all I have.

I rode Gemmy weekends and holidays for three years until I sold the saddle I'd saved up for and bought the 10-speed bike I rode through James Smith's Department Store. I fell off that quite a lot. Sigh.

Somewhere along the line I became a journalist, which is actually quite extraordinary because I always thought I was going to be a vet, and I have UE Physics, Maths, Biology and Chemistry to prove it.

I must have sent my application form off to the wrong place because I ended up at Wellington Polytechnic doing the journalism course, and I was most the way through the year before I realised I had yet to stick my hand up an animal's arse. I was pretty much a hopeless flop at Journalism School, excelling only at typing and shorthand, and that was just because my Aunty Irene was the teacher and everytime I failed a test she made me stay behind at lunchtime and do revision with her.

The year was not wasted though. And by the time I picked up my sad and sorry diploma at the end of it, I had several close friends in the nearby Graphic Design school. By the time my certificate was winging its way to the country's newspapers and radio stations, it was sporting a whole lot more B-pluses than it had started out with, and a whole lot fewer E-minuses.

I am quick to add I am far from proud of this story, but especially because even with that expert forgery, I could still only get a job as a cub reporter on the *Taupo Times*. Or the *Taupo-Behind-The-Times* as it was cruelly dubbed. And yes, it was located in Taupo. I bumped into the former editor of the *Taupo Times* at a flash do recently, and because I had regaled a couple of audiences with this jolly jape and feared it might get back to him, I decided to come clean.

'I've got a confession to make if you promise there'll be no repercussions,' I wheedled over curry and rice at the Ellerslie Racecourse.

'Go ahead,' he nodded.

'I forged my certificate to get that job at the *Taupo Times*,' I blurted.

'Well, I'm not surprised,' he came back, unruffled. 'You forged your driver's licence to hire a rental car, too, as I remember.' My goodness, even I hadn't remembered that. What I did remember was that when I Left the *Taupo Times* to continue my career in Palmerston North (if I ever look like doing that again, please slap me), this same man had said to me: 'You'd have had a lot more fun here if you liked hunting and shooting and fishing.' Well, yes. He had a point. But I was never the hunting and shooting and fishing type. There was no form of physical activity, in fact, in which I could glean even the smallest amount of fun.

In my early 20s, though, I stumbled upon Jazzercise. At the time I thought I was hideously fat although, as I've said before, I would give the two middle rolls on my tummy to be that fat now. I had tried Weightwatchers again, and while that seemed to be going nowhere in a hurry there was a greater emphasis on exercise this time around, so I decided to give Jazzercise a shot.

Stuff It!

How like being back at Miss Sebastian Cabot's it seemed. I turned up wearing trainers, baggy tracksuit pants, a holey T-shirt and grubby sweatshirt. Well, why would you bother looking good for exercise? Perhaps it has something to do with all those mirrors. Anyway, by the time I had found a place in the vast, packed room where I couldn't see my own reflection, the class was well underway and no matter how hard I tried, I couldn't catch up. It seemed that just as I'd got the hang of doing a 'grapevine' to the left, everyone was doing them to the right, and while I was still marching forward, everyone else was going backwards. Wherever I was, there seemed a small crowd of people bumping into each other. The glares were frightening and I'm sure someone was scratching me on purpose. My cheeks burned with embarrassment — or was it the pain of doing bicycles? When it came time to do press-ups, I couldn't lift anything off the floor, not even my head. Still, I liked jiggling around to the music, and as I was a frustrated ballerina I decided to keep going.

Thus began my love-hate relationship with aerobics.

Not long after this introduction, I moved to Sydney and got a job as a sub-editor at *CLEO* magazine, the glossy monthly for young females, despite grossly exaggerating my subbing skills during the interview process. I strongly suspect that I got the job because I was a Kurt Vonnegut fan at the time, as was the Chief Sub, and when you think about it, that's probably more of a sign that you're going to get on with each other than anything else.

On the whole, working at *CLEO* was a bitter disappointment. I had imagined that it would be all big hair, sharp fingernails and lunches, darling, lunches, but really it was dead boring. Also, being a lowly sub on a monthly magazine means that you get to read every single story about 55 times before it's printed. Truly, the things I don't know about orgasm and rejection would fit on a condom wrapper!

Once I spent a whole week abridging a Harold Robbins novel from around 200,000 words to 10,000. I had to read it four times before I could start working out what bits to chop out, and by the Wednesday I had done it, but being oversensitive to our readers' squeamishness, I had removed all mention of sex. Unfortunately, this left only words like 'and', 'to', 'from', 'heave' and 'slam'. I spent the Thursday putting the sexy bits back. I am still tortured by the memory of one reference at the end of the book when the man and the woman who have hated each other all the way through end up staying together in the same room. Finally, out of nowhere, she demands, 'Get those shorts off, or I'll rip them off,' which he immediately does, to the reverberating sound of his phallus slapping against his stomach. It brought tears to a young girl's eyes, I can tell you.

Now here's a little how-rich-people-get-that-way story I'm sure you will love. While I was at *CLEO*, Gretel Packer came to work there. Gretel is Kerry Packer's daughter. Kerry Packer owned the company. Gretel has since been married in a million dollar ceremony in Britain and is probably living in a castle somewhere with a thousand servants, but at the time she was a lowly assistant in the fashion department. One day Gretel rushed into work clutching a cappuccino she'd bought on the way in to work. Unfortunately for her, the fashion team was on its way out somewhere and there was no time for her to have a coffee.

'Does anybody want this cappuccino?' she asked our department.

'Oooh, yes — I'll have it,' volunteered one of the subs.

'That's a dollar fifty,' said Gretel. And she wasn't joking.

Most people who worked at *CLEO* were obsessed with food one way or another. To begin with, I was obsessed with eating quite a lot of it, especially as the food halls near where we worked were a veritable smorgasbord of foreign delicacies, the likes of which I had not encountered in New Zealand. The Lebanese food in particular in Sydney was superlative — falafels and kebabs were my favourites. However, other *CLEO* staff members were obsessed with eating not very much food. There were a couple of vegetarians who never talked about anything else, and would unload the most unappetising but complicated salad collections in the kitchen at lunchtime. While it drove me mad, I couldn't escape noticing the fact that they were both thin.

I was getting depressed about not being able to squeeze into size 14s again at this stage, so decided to keep a food diary. Imagine my horror when I developed writer's cramp after only a week. I decided then that I would only write down the foods that I wouldn't mind reading about afterwards, but after a week of that, it seemed pointless, especially as I was believing what was in my food diary rather than what was in my stomach and was therefore genuinely surprised I wasn't losing weight.

Then, one of the skinny *CLEO* vegetarians introduced me to the gym. It was owned by Kerry Packer too (wasn't everything?), and was in the building right next door. It was quite posh and quite expensive but as an employee perk, your membership could be taken automatically out of your wages so you'd hardly notice.

My first fitness assessment was pretty depressing. Having not weighed myself for several years I was more than a little shocked to find out I weighed 95 kilos — don't even try to work it out in stones. Do you think I would tell you what it was if it was in stones? Can't you just be happy with the fact that it's a lot of kilos?

My fitness level was off the bottom of the graph and my body fat was off the top. Apparently, it was a wonder I could move. The shock of all this just about did me in, so I went off to the doctor the next day to get some more diet pills. Yes, that's what I needed! From then on I threw myself into exercising and not eating. And I mean exercising and not eating.

Every morning, I would get up and go and do an aerobics class before work. Then I'd have my breakfast at my desk, sort of mid-morning so I wouldn't have to have lunch. That would consist of fresh fruit, yoghurt and bran. Then at lunchtime I would go to the gym again. Sometimes I'd swim in the pool, sometimes do another aerobics class, sometimes do weights. Then after work I would go back and do another aerobics class or have another swim or do another weights session.

Then I would go home and have dinner. Either broccoli or grapes. At the weekend I would come into town for long sessions at the gym. I would not go out. I would rarely see my friends. I only wanted to exercise and not eat. After the first month, I didn't even need the diet pills any more. After six months, I weighed 70 kilos.

Finally, on the day Sarah Ferguson married Prince Andrew, a very old and dear friend of mine rang me up at work and yelled at me for being such a screw-up. She did her best to snap me out of my coma, and I did go and watch the nuptials and feast on finger food that night, but the next day I was back at the gym for two aerobics sessions to purge the phyllo pastry before it stayed forever on my hips.

In case you think weighing 70 kilos brought me instant happiness — *au contraire, mon frère*. I still couldn't get the boy-friends I wanted, and the boyfriends that wanted me were like zombies. Plus, it's quite hard to keep not eating anything and exercising a lot, because if you let either slip you're in trouble pretty quickly.

When a friend of mine rang up from a small tourist town in New Zealand and asked me to come back and look after her PR business while she returned to Europe for a few months I jumped at the chance. When I got there, I was completely devastated to find that there wasn't a gym. For the third time I tried running — and vomited. I was so distressed that I couldn't eat more than one small packet of peanuts a day for fear of putting on weight.

The only good thing about being there at all was that nobody knew I had been fat. To all intents and purposes, I was a thin person. This was my big chance to drop the baggage of excess weight I had been carrying around with me, and act like all the other girls.

I fell in love with someone else's boyfriend.

The someone else didn't take too kindly to this.

The boyfriend stuck with the someone else.

Stuff It!

Somehow, one packet of peanuts a day just wasn't enough any more.

And I thought being skinny would solve all my problems! I moved back to Wellington and began my close personal friendship with fish and chips once more. To be honest, it's not that hard to eat your way back to 95 kilos when you've been surviving on peanuts and broccoli for a year.

I've continued my love-hate relationship with aerobics ever since, though. Only enough to gain me a Below Average fitness rating of course, but hey, who wants to be average?

- 9 -
I've been a round in the world

In which it is proved that there is nowhere in the world
where it is truly fabulous to be truly enormous
— thanks largely to the King of Tonga

BY MY LATE 20s I had come to the conclusion that possibly the only way I was ever going to feel great about the shape I came in was by finding a country where corpulence was seen as a sign of enormous intelligence and great superiority.

I looked, but I never did find such a place, so if you can point me in the right direction please do — now would be good. I did think for a while that Tonga might be the place because I read somewhere that the King of Tonga took up three seats on an aeroplane and where he came from, the bigger you were the more respect you commanded. Finding out about him was a great weight off my mind (no where else, mind you) because it got me out of my dilemma over constantly seeking people who were fatter than me. My one worry over this method of temporarily feeling thin was that if the people who were fatter than me were in turn seeking people fatter than them it was all eventually going to go horribly wrong the day the fattest person of all couldn't find anyone fatter. He or she was going to feel very, very bad that day and it was going to be partly my fault. Correct? Well, this is where the King of Tonga fitted in. Here was the fattest man in the whole, wide world and not only did he not give a fat rat's butt about how many seats he took up, he was the king of something! Excellent. He could take the pressure of all the other fat guys.

Sadly, the lo-fat Nazis have gotten to the old Kay of Tee in recent years and he has halved his bulk, leaving that particular theory down the gurgler — but it was good while it lasted.

Anyway, when I hit 27 and set off on my inevitable Overseas Experience, the first city I arrived in was Amsterdam, and I have to say this is one of my favourite food cities in the world. Hello, we are talking about a country that sprinkles chocolate hail on its toast for breakfast — yes, it's true.

I know most people love Amsterdam because they can smoke their brains out and not get into trouble, well, with the police, anyway, but I tell you the food is something else.

I was staying with a New Zealand friend who had lived in Amsterdam for some years and was fond of a snack himself, so I was in excellent company. Our breakfasts would consist of rye bread, cheeses, ham, eggs, and a selection of chocolate hails that was really our reason for getting up in the morning.

Lunch would always be frites, which might have had a fancy French name but were still chips to me, and you know how I just love a fried potato. These were served up in a big paper cone (OK, mine were in a big cone, but you could get them in small and medium too) and were cooked to perfection — larger than a McDonalds fry but smaller than the local chippie — and were topped off, nay, perfected, by the biggest, fattest dollop of Belgian mayonnaise, made with eggs, that you ever did savour. Now, I know they say that Belgium is the five most boring countries in the world, but man, do they know how to make mayonnaise, and beer, and chocolates.

Actually, I was on a train going through Belgium to get from

Amsterdam to London once, when it stopped suddenly and stayed that way. After two hours I finally found a red-faced train guard who, when I gesticulated wildly and threw my hands about in a 'What gives, Hercule Poirot?' sort of a fashion, replied, 'I speak no English. The train has killed a man.' Which is my little interesting story that I have about Belgium that I bring out on occasions such as this.

You know, just thinking about those frites has got me in a lather, but there was one other taste sensation in Amsterdam that actually surpassed my special spuds. I'm talking about deep-fried peanut butter. This is probably not the Dutch name for this delicacy but, ooooooh, words barely do it justice at all, so what does it matter. Throughout the main tourist areas of Amsterdam are fast-food joints that offer up a wall of small glass windows behind which lie the most fantastic treats the saliva can imagine. Simply drop the correct number of guilders in the slot and the windows pop open so you can reach in and grab your heart's desire. Then a mysterious hand behind the wall will replace your little friend with another. I could probably get in the *Guinness Book of Records* for my devotion to deep-fried peanut butter and you know, the truth is, those little crumbed, fried objects are mainly the reason why I keep returning to Amsterdam.

Never mind smoking your brains out and wandering the streets and canals in a haze of drug-induced hilarity and confusion until finally you find a seat outside a place called the Maybe Bar, only to sit there for hours until you realise that Maybe it is never going to open and hey, your fingers look funny. Yes. Well. Anyway.

After Amsterdam, I moved on to London, to a flat above a bakery in Shepherd's Bush. As it turns out, if there is one place above which I should not live, it is a bakery. I don't have a particularly sweet tooth so how I developed such an addiction to custard doughnuts I do not know, but they told me at the Betty Ford Clinic that my withdrawal symptoms made Elizabeth Taylor's look like wind.

Stuff It!

Within a month of arriving in England I had moved out of my jeans and into elasticated waistbands, big time. It's a fate that strikes many a New Zealand lass, and I remember a discussion among staff at the *Woman's Weekly* in which it was revealed that everybody in the room who had lived in London had put on two stone while doing so.

I think the blame should fall fair and square at the foot of the greasy spoon, myself. This, thankfully, is a concept that has not caught on over here; it involves small cafés on every corner serving up a variety of deep-fried foodstuffs accompanied by strong, barely drinkable, I'd-better-add-some-sugar tea. This sort of food is extremely cheap and extremely comforting, and seems to occur largely at lunchtimes, which does nothing for an antipodean girl's waistline.

I also found the English a nation of great potato crisp eaters and hey, when in yadder yadder, do what the yadderer yadderers do. Isn't that how the saying goes? That, combined with the huge quantities of beer it seems mandatory to drink, is certainly not conducive to weight loss or even, it seems, stability.

Another country I love for its food is Greece, mostly because everything comes with feta cheese. Breakfast is the thickest, creamiest yoghurt with honey and bread; lunch is an enormous Greek salad with lashings of olive oil and a mountain of bread; and dinner is lamb or chicken or fish cooked pretty much anyway you like it. Of course, I love moussaka — well, who wouldn't? Anything with cheese sauce has got to be good for you. Have I got that right?

After one such delicious feast in a town called Sitia on the island of Crete, my husband had the good sense to abandon my friend Justine and I, who had both developed a fearful thirst for retsina. After several hours consuming said paint stripper on a balcony overlooking the port we attempted to stagger up the unfurl-the-flag-sherpa hill to the cheap hotel where we were staying.

I'm sorry to report that by this stage it was the wee smalls of the morning and we were clutching each other in a tired and emotional fashion crying, 'I love you Justine' and 'I love you Sarah-Kate' at each other when we walked past a lively sounding restaurant with three elderly men keeping post at the door.

Well, within the blink of an eye (most likely unintentional but you never know with Justine) we were sitting inside, sandwiched between crumbly old Cretans drinking their ouzo (excellent idea on top of your own bodyweight in retsina, must try that again sometime — perhaps when my stomach lining grows back) and smoking their fags (another top international idea I'm desperate to repeat). Once the music started up, I grabbed the oldest looking one among them — who would have been 150 if he was a day and appeared to be wearing a pacemaker on the outside of his body — and whisked him onto the dance floor where I proceeded to tantalise him with the hustle, the bump and other alluring movements totally inappropriate to what I later realised was obviously a family occasion to celebrate someone's thousandth birthday.

Justine, who's always been a bit of a strumpet on the dance floor, then proceeded to do her John Travolta with cleavage impersonations with a 149-year-old, which proved the final straw for the assorted wives and mothers in the room who in our torpor we had actually failed to notice up until that moment.

Never have you seen a sock put in the music so quickly. Then the wives and mothers lined up facing ourselves and the over-excited old crumblies and started shouting all at once in words we did not understand, but the gist being get us the hell out of their faces or it would be souvlakis at dawn.

For a while the geriatrics defended us by banding together and singing back in unison at their screaming womenfolk, but then they got nervous and started hustling us towards the door. We staggered up the hill laughing and giggling, and it wasn't until the next morning that we realised what terrible oiks we had made of ourselves. Well, actually, Justine didn't realise it till the next evening as she couldn't get out of bed until 6 p.m.

My next most favourite country for food is America, mostly because I had a miraculous weight-losing experience there and those are pretty thin on the ground on the whole.

When I flew into New York City I didn't own anything that didn't come on an elastic waistband. When I flew out of LA a month later, I was wearing black jeans, a tight-fitting top and I practically had hip bones, and do you know who I have to thank — McDonalds, that's who.

I was travelling with one of my favourite cousins, Dave, and our aim was to have as many adventures as possible, and I have to say our strike rate was pretty good although most of the adventures cannot be repeated here, suffice to say one of them even involved being practically held at gunpoint by a deranged Vietnam vet fresh out of jail from shooting his brother-in-law in the stomach ('Well, I didn't kill him or nuthin"), and keen to enlist our help in extorting some Class A drugs from a Florida crack-house.

Note to myself: remember never to travel with favourite cousin Dave again.

Dave and I had found out pretty much early on in the trip that neither of us had a sense of direction and neither of us could read a map and neither of us could make a decision, the combination of which meant we spent a lot of time dithering until Dave saw an old episode of 'Bonanza' one afternoon and Boss Cartwright sadly told an ancient Irish sot named Danny Lynch who was drifting through the Ponderosa that, 'You don't need a plan to lean against a bar, Danny', which Dave took as some kind of omen and introduced as the motto for our trip.

Anyway, in a first for me, eating was low on our list of priorities as we drove across the States in various cars which we were delivering to their owners. Because we had delivery deadlines to meet, we used to drive in long stretches and pretty soon we started eating exclusively at McDonalds. The amazing thing about these restaurants is that wherever you go they are exactly the same. I mean, you never even have to ask where the bathroom is because it's in the exact same place it was in the other McDonalds back down the road some.

Sometimes we would just stop for coffee, and sometimes I would have a salad, which are absolutely delicious in the McDonalds over there and you *know* I am not a salad fan. They came with big chunks of chicken and croutons (OK, so I was only in it for the croutons, so sue me) and by week two, stateside, were all I was eating.

After the Vietnam vet incident, we stayed pretty much in our hotel room jumping around singing 'We're alive, we're alive', leaving only to pick up a rental car and attend a football game at the Miami Bowl where the hometown's Dolphins were playing the Cleveland Browns. (The Dolphins had much better uniforms, by the way.) When we came to leave the Bowl, I asked Dave where we had parked the car. Of course, he didn't know. Then I asked him what kind of car it was. Of course, he didn't know that either. Colour? Forget it. Needless to say we had to wait till the other 60,000 people went home before we could identify our vehicle, and we didn't even have a bar to lean on in the meantime. Hungered by this nerve-wracking experience we stopped at a McDonalds on the way back to the hotel and were already at the front of the queue before we realised we were the only white people in there.

'You from Canada?' demanded the enormous black woman behind the counter with a ruby set in her front tooth.

'No,' I squeaked, knowing that Canada is the next most boring five countries after Belgium.

'Had someone else in here spoke like you once,' she glared. 'She was from Canada.'

Several days and states later, in New Mexico, I received an offer of marriage in a McDonalds. By this stage, I was actually getting a warm feeling in my tummy and my head whenever I saw the golden arches. I still do. Thanks Mackers.

We'd travelled through Texas — yes everything is bigger there — stopping at places like the only known Elvis Presley Memorial Taco Stand in Austin, where I had bought a T-shirt which I was wearing on my way back from the counter in McDonald's in New Mexico.

'Hey, little lady,' boomed a grey-bearded old man in denim dungarees who looked just like the grandfather in the 'Dukes of Hazzard', 'now what part of Texas do you come from?'

'I come from the New Zealand part, actually,' I replied, and then spent several minutes explaining to him what New Zealand was and why I would come from there. When he established that we were on our way to LA Grandpaw became quite excitable and started talking about the sea and surf and sand that we would find there. Pegging me obviously as a desperate spinster he added encouragingly, 'I'd marry you myself if you were staying round these parts, but go to LA and you'll find a husband half my age.'

'And with twice the amount of legs,' Dave added dolefully as we watched Grandpaw pick his dungarees out of his prosthesis at the door as he left.

Do you know the only person to ever ask me to marry them apart from my husband (and I told him to ask me) was that one-legged old hillbilly in McDonalds. No wonder the filet of fish still means so much to me.

Once we arrived in LA eating was the last thing on my mind because you do not want to carry extra weight in a town where even a stick lying on the side of the road goes to aerobics and has a tan.

We quickly got involved in another adventure involving a bikie, a homeless person and large amounts of Russian beer, and were recovering in our West Hollywood hotel (Econolodge — spend a night not a fortune) when I decided to go shopping for supplies at the local market two blocks down on Vine (that's how they talk over there).

I gathered all I needed in my arms, lo-fat Tylenol for headaches, lo-fat water for hydration, lo-fat crackers for lager sponge, lo-fat Reece's Peanut Butter Cups (yeah, right!), lo-fat magazines, etc., and headed to the least congested check-out, where a huge, furious-looking black woman wearing the name badge 'Dolores' was shoving convenience foods in a brown paper sack for the person in front of me.

I started to off-load my goods onto the counter when Dolores' head snapped back, her eyes rolling around at the front of it, and she shouted, 'Do not place your items on the counter until the person in front of you has completed their purchase.' Frankly, Dolores did not look like the sort of person you would want to be duffed up by in the carpark later on so, red-faced, I gathered all my bits and pieces up in my arms again and stood there waiting, like I was told to.

Next thing, a little squirt of a guy comes along and gets in the queue behind me. He too, has an armful of stuff, which he too starts to unload onto the counter. I bulge my eyes at him by way of warning, but since he's not looking at me, it's not much help.

Sure enough, Dolores' head snaps back, eyes roll, she shouts, 'Do not place your items on the counter until the person in front of you has completed their purchase!'

Well, I'm standing there quaking in my boots, hanging onto my armful of lo-fat for grim death because I know, deep down, hey, I know it on the surface, that this is not a woman to piss off. But the little guy looks at me, he looks at her, he looks at her badge, he looks at me again, then he looks her straight in the eye and he says, 'Screw you, Dolores,' and leaves the store.

Now that's an attitude.

- 10 -
The top ten excuses for being fat

1. It's glandular

2. I never lost weight after the baby
   (NB, Particularly useful if you never had a baby)

3. I'm not me, I'm my much fatter sister

4. I ate New York

5. I'm allergic to everything except meat pies
   and potato crisps

6. I left my body in my other suit

7. I used to jog but the ice kept falling out of the glass

8. Compared to the King of Tonga, I'm actually not that fat

9. I eat too much and I never exercise

10. Screw you, Dolores!

- 11 -
Our friend the elastic waistband

***A look at the torture of finding clothes to wear
if you're not Cindy Crawford which,
I must point out, most of us aren't***

NOT BEING ABLE to fit nice clothes is by far the worst part of being overweight.

The only times I have ever really been totally, sobbingly, miserable about the whole business are when I've been sitting on the end of my bed staring at my wardrobe, knowing deep down that nothing in it could possibly make me look even the slightest bit like Elle McPherson.

Like most people who have long battled the bulge, my wardrobe usually consists of three different elements: my fat clothes, the clothes I'm wearing now, and my thin clothes. It doesn't matter how fat or thin you are, by the way, those three elements remain constant. There is also usually a pair of trousers used as a control to establish which phase of your wardrobe you are currently in.

Fat clothes are loose and flowing and make you look enormous but you don't feel so bad if you're having a fat day because they don't pinch or restrain you in any way. The clothes you are wearing now pinch or restrain you if you are having a fat day. The thin clothes? Yeah, right, like you can get anywhere near any of those.

I'm trying to cut down on my fat and thin wardrobes these days because it suddenly occurred to me one day that I will never again see the inside of the pair of Levi's I've been waiting to fit in to for about eight years. I mean, we'll be wearing the matching all-in-one silver space suits by the time I get near them again, if you know what I'm saying.

So, I've taken the brave and courageous stand of removing them from the wardrobe and hiding them in the musty trunk in the spare room. That took guts, I can tell you. Maybe in another eight years I'll throw them away altogether, or make a patchwork quilt out of them and all my other musty smelling thin clothes. A lot of my other fat and thin clothes I sold to a shop, and with the proceeds had a really nice suit made that fits me perfectly, and because it was made especially it does not have a size on it.

Sizing is a real problem once you're over 14. A size 16, psychologically, is bad for your esteem, even though most women are over it. Now how did this ever come to be? Why don't the people who make clothes change the sizes so that an 18 becomes a 12 because the old 12s are not going to mind that they are now 6s but the 20s will be ecstatic at being 14s. Doesn't this make perfect sense?

Instead, anyone with lumps and bumps has to finger sadly through the squitty 14s at Country Road — knowing they'll never get them over their thighs even if they are on elastic waistbands — then go to the fat ladies' shop if they dare. Personally, I do not dally in the fat ladies' departments. Partly because that means I'd be a fat lady (yeah, and I'm keeping that a secret), and partly because the clothes are often not just bigger versions of the thin ladies' clothes but are special cuts just for fat ladies and I don't like them. I would rather wear leggings and men's linen shirts than some of the sofa covers I've seen for sale in these places.

I suppose it's just another lesson in sticking with what you know, never mind your inbuilt desire to be a normal size 14 despite the size 18 dimension of your hips. Now I am no style queen (you don't *have* to agree with me on that), but I think I have sometimes captured the essence of dressing to look less fat than I actually am, and my recipe for doing so has been simple. No patterns and no pale colours. In fact, dressing all in black is one of the best diets I've ever been on, and I didn't even have to go to the gym.

It all started when I was about 17 and a friend of mine was trying to talk me into going somewhere, probably a slap-up feast at the Mexican Cantina — and I didn't want to go because I was having a fat year. She was no smaller than me, in fact bigger, but very blonde and not someone who wore her weight like a sack of spuds around her neck — I hardly noticed it and obviously neither did the local lads, the advances of whom she spent much of her time beating off with a big stick. Anyway, her response when I said I couldn't go because I was on a diet was, 'Bugger the diet, wear black', which I've pretty much done ever since, and I know that this has worked well for me because when I deviate from it, people let me know.

'Lose the beige linen skirt, it does nothing for you,' a particularly forthright friend told me recently. Actually the only reason I had the beige linen skirt in the first place was because it was the only thing from Country Road that ever fitted me, and that is not enough of a reason. I lost the beige linen skirt.

But at least I *could* lose the beige linen skirt. In the dreadful Disgusting Outfit Disaster of 1987 I had not been so lucky as to escape my heinous clothing.

One hot summer morning I was meandering through Wellington's Cuba Mall (there are so hot summer mornings in Wellington) on my way to a reporting shift due to start at the local radio station at noon.

Stuff It!

Even though it was already 11.30, I couldn't resist the desire to try on unsuitable clothing in an ethnic clothes shop, mostly because, due to a number of circumstances, I happened to be very badly dressed. I had stayed the night at a friend's house and, as it should be, his supply of clean women's knickers was a bit thin on the ground so I was forced to wear a pair of his own knickers. The only ones I could truly trust were an unopened pair of boxer shorts I myself had given him for Christmas. They were white cotton with enormous black polka dots and in the event of a nasty road accident aspersions would no doubt be cast on my character for wearing them but, hey, I wasn't going to do that turning yesterday's inside-out thing, either. Anyway, by the time I had my jeans on over them, who'd know?

Sadly, because of the sweltering heat of the day, a sudden desire to be wearing something much cooler propelled me towards the ethnic clothes shop. My eyes alighted on a flimsy white muslin smock dress that, had I had all my marbles with me, I would have flitted straight past. But no, into the changing room we went.

Ten minutes later I was still trying to get my cowboy boots off. They were only a matter of weeks old, and I had bought them at a shop on Melrose Avenue in Los Angeles which claimed to also clad the feet of George Michael. I guess I should have known that they were going to be trouble when even in the shop the only way to get them on was by first putting plastic bags on my feet. Truthfully, I could never get them off that easily on my own and often had to enlist the help of at least one strong young man to help me (that was my story and I'm sticking to it). There were no such strong young men here with me in the cubicle, though. Grr. I bet George Michael didn't have this trouble. Man, it was hot in here. Thanks to my boot removal programme I had rivulets of sweat running down my sides trying to make a break for freedom. Finally, after much pulling and groaning, the sodding footwear shot off, so I removed my socks and slipped on the see-through smock. I wasn't 100 per cent certain, but I was pretty sure it looked like a very old dish rag stretched over a large brown rock with a black tree on top. Still, at least it fit, and you couldn't tell anything with these pokey mirrors, anyway — I would have to venture out. But venturing out barefoot was not done, not by me anyway, and especially in an ethnic dress shop. What about verucas?

Now, here's where my marbles eluded me altogether. Disregarding my socks I wrenched the cowboy boots on to my bare sweaty feet and went outside for a look in the mirror. It was not a pretty sight. The dress was suited really only to a pregnant midget, an altar boy or a mechanic who might use it every now and then to get the oil off his hands or open a boiling hot radiator cap. On a tall, curvy, crabby journalist wearing George Michael's cowboy boots it looked like the remains of an old tea towel thrown out of the window by a furious fishwife. What was worse, the polka dot boxer shorts were plain as day beneath the flimsy muslin and drew more attention to the child-bearing potential of my hips than you would otherwise have thought possible.

I had to take this hideous garment off — immediately. Back in the cubicle removing the dress was a breeze, but when it came time to replace said frock with my jeans, I had a problem. My boots. At this stage it was ten past the time I was supposed to start work, and there I was sweating to death in a stuffy cubicle wearing nothing but a tasteless pair of boxer shorts, the smell of joss sticks burning a hole in my head and my boots uncommon attached to my feet. The socks! Why were they lying in a lump on the floor instead of lubricating the inside of these torture chambers? I hopped and pulled, pulled and hopped, sat on the floor and wrenched, wrenched, wrenched, but at 12.20 those blasted boots had moved not an inch. Where was a strong young man when you needed one? That waif-like hippy examining cannabis smoking apparatus at the counter would be no help to me whatsoever, even if I did swallow my pride and ask her to help. Without first removing my boots, I could not put on my jeans. Without my jeans I was only wearing my boots and a pair of ill-fitting boxer shorts. Trust me, this was not a good look. There was only one thing for it. Back on went the see-through dishcloth and $40 later I was clomping my way towards work looking like 'something dressed out of the Corso bag', as my mother would say, only worse, because my huge black polka dots shimmered around my hips as I walked, clearly visible through the skimpy overlayer.

In case you think I exaggerate the ugliness of this outfit, the eyeballs of my colleague fair bulged out of her head when I turned up at work, and she was moved to comment on my unattractive appearance. However, being of small stature and slender build she was not a likely candidate for boot removal, and we simply decided I should stay hidden from the world until going home time, when the help of strong young men could again be enlisted.

To this end, I had hoped to remain in the confines of the radio station doing my work by phone and therefore not exposing myself to the public in general, but sadly this was not to be. Finance Minister Roger Douglas had recently resigned and Radio New Zealand Head Office had it on good authority he was arriving at Wellington airport in half an hour's time, so could I please go there and get some comment from him on tape. Now I have tried before using being badly dressed as an excuse for poor performance in the workplace. (I was once an hour late after being thrown into confusion about what to wear when my skirt proved too tight to enable me to ride my bike to work. This was actually true, but I now realise I would have gotten more sympathy from my boss with a well constructed lie.) I just hoped that I could slip in and out of the domestic terminal totally unnoticed.

How my cheeks burned with shame when I pounced on Roger at the airport, only for the two of us to be in turn pounced on by not one television film crew but two. Cameras? Cameras! Everywhere! And me in my billowing polka dots, dwarfing poor little Rog in my sails as I thrust my microphone under his nose and my tape recorder in front of my privates where I knew the dots would be doing their worst. We sailed towards the exit under the glare of the camera lights, and do you think I can remember a word of what was said?

That night I turned on the six o'clock news and to my horror there was Roger and his nomics, the lead item, with me and my enormous polka dot pants playing second fiddle in a most unattractive way. I could only be thankful that I wasn't bundled into a van at the airport and sent off immediately to the Home for Tilted People. An hour later the phone rang and a journalist colleague of mine was still choking with laughter so much he could barely get out his line about wearing the sign off the rewind button. And yet, my humiliation was not over.

Roger Douglas immediately went to ground and could not be found again for comment. As a result, every time a TV reporter wanted pictures of him to flesh out a story, he or she would go to the TVNZ library and get the most recent available footage of the little man arriving that day at Wellington airport.

For months I was haunted by those polka dot pants and those bloody boots. The dress became an oil rag overnight, and rightly so.

I am happy to report there is no smocked white muslin in my wardrobe these days. It now consists of a selection of men's linen shirts, some coloured, some black, some white; several pairs of black jodhpurs; one pair of jeans; a black dress and three black suits I had specially made, a black leather jacket and a huge selection of black exercise wear which lies mangled up in a heap I never look at.

I do have, in a bottom drawer with all my scarves that I never wear, a black, stretch-knit, lace-up clingy T-shirt top from Joseph, the London shop where all the supermodels buy their clothes.

Actually, when I was in there myself (after explaining to the security guard that I wasn't a bag lady, just a simply dressed tourist, a fact he did not seem to comprehend until after I removed a fiver from myself), who should I find fingering her way up the aisles but Kylie Minogue. My first response was to go and stand as close to her as I could to establish whether she was as pint-sized as she always looked in pictures. She was. My thigh was bigger than her waist and further off the ground too, I might add. Kylie couldn't find anything small enough to wear so she tried to buy one of the display cabinets, probably so she could sleep in a drawer should she fall on hard times.

Anyway, I bought my Joseph top which now lives in my scarf drawer and fits into that other category of clothing called Things I'll Buy Now To Encourage Me To Get Thin So I Can Actually Wear Them.

These differ from the Levi's you've been waiting eight years to fit into because you will never, ever wear these clothes. If you do, they will be too small for you and you will feel very uncomfortable and never wear them again, and probably never even be able to go back to the place that you wore them to and will also have to drop the friends you went there with to boot. They are that much too small for you.

I have had whole wardrobes of these clothes before. I once went on a shopping spree in a department store in San Francisco (once is the number of times I have been to San Fransisco, actually), and in one hour I bought hundreds of dollars of clothes which did not fit me.

I brought them back home where they sat in my wardrobe with their sale tags hanging off them, and I'd see them and think, 'I'll be wearing you soon'. After three years, I got rid of them. Now all that remains is that Joseph top, and that is different because I really will fit into that one day. No, really, I will. I said I will. Somebody, slap me, please.

I have a theory about how shoes can make you look thinner, too, but it may only apply to my particular type of leg; however, this theory, which is mine, is that legs are big at the top, smaller in the middle, and even smaller at the end. Now (this is the important part of the theory) to avoid your legs looking like ice cream cones, which is very unflattering to the thigh, *wear clompy shoes.*

(It's important to note at this stage that you should avoid other advice about this kind of footwear such as — and this was offered up by the Welsh mother of a friend of mine overseas — 'You will never find a husband wearing those clompy shoes.' A wonderful woman now, sadly, gone, she also once asked me if the Maoris' grass skirts ever got stuck in car doors.)

There is nothing scientific in my theory (no, really) except that somehow the balancing of a solid thigh with a clompy shoe flatters the leg in between. I am lucky in that I have been blessed with a slender area from my shin to my ankle. Hey! I know it's not much but still, I'm grateful. In fact, my late father used to joke it was a wonder my ankles could hold the rest of me up. He was convinced my weight problem was the result of biting my fingernails since I was a tiny baby, and since fingernails didn't break down they probably just backed up around your body and gave you lumps. When I explained that this was not an opinion backed up by research or shared by the dieting fraternity he replied with his favourite saying; 'Opinions are like arseholes — everyone's got one and they all think the other guys' stinks.'

The shoes only have to be of a clompiness to suit the style of the owner of the thigh. I wear great, big, black clompy shoes with thick one-inch heels, but women who wear more ladylike shoes could stick with high heels as long as the heel is thick and clompy, not stilletto. Go on, try it — I dare you to. Remember: ice cream cones are great if there's ice cream on top of them — but not so great if you are on top of them.

My clompy shoe theory ties in with another theory of mine that you can tell a lot about people by the sort of shoes they wear. For example, I have never met a man wearing grey, vinyl zip-ups who has not been trying to sell me a used car or some insurance. I have never met a woman wearing Charlie Browns and baggy flesh-coloured tights who is not still at home living with her mother. I have never met anyone wearing knitted roller skates who is not a newborn baby. You see? I rest my case.

The other theory I have is that for some reason having flabby underarms is worse than having a flabby anything else. It's funny when Bette Midler makes her flabby triceps swing with the breeze, but I have tried this myself at dinner parties and met with a very different response — i.e. everyone screaming and running from the room. As the years go by and clothes get smaller and smaller, it gets harder and harder to buy garments that do not reveal this part of your personage. Sleeveless clothes are filling the shelves in their thousands, taunting and daring those whose cellulite does not limit itself to the thigh.

Speaking of cellulite, I heard a nightmare story from a very dear friend of mine with whom I have spent many, many hours discussing the thicker points of having child-bearing hips, pot bellies and orange-peel thighs. She once rushed back from a summer holiday in the early stages of a hot romance to tell me she had been sitting on the beach with her loved one when he scanned the crowds of skimpily dressed strumpets, turned to her, scanned the strumpets again, then turned back to her. 'Tell me,' he asked suddenly, 'what are all those little holes in your thighs and why haven't the other girls got them?' Luckily you can fib your head off when someone has read so few women's magazines, and she got away with telling him it's where the angels touched her when she was a baby, or something like that. Goodness, what a close shave! It's a miracle they are now a happily married couple.

I'm not even going to delve any further into the subject of cellulite because despite my constant kilo concertina routine, I don't have it. Unless, of course, it lurks underneath the kilos I currently carry. Or would that just be too much like bad luck?

Well, while I'm waiting to see if my cellulite ever comes to the surface, I may as well wait for the leg o' mutton sleeve to come back in so I can put my leg o' mutton arm in it.

- 12 -
The you-can't-write-a-book-about-stomachs-and-not-mention-sex-chapter

In which I think the heading says it all, don't you?

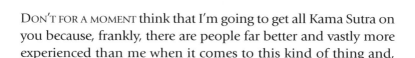

DON'T FOR A MOMENT think that I'm going to get all Kama Sutra on you because, frankly, there are people far better and vastly more experienced than me when it comes to this kind of thing and, besides, I'm giving my mother a copy of this book for Christmas.

I simply want to point out a few home truths about the missionary position.

I know you blokes think we prefer it because we're completely useless and mentally compiling a list of ten top Hollywood hearthrobs, lying back and thinking of Mother England, or lying back and thinking of different ways to make non-fattening canapés look attractive, but the sad truth is that we're actually lying back thinking of our stomachs.

You see, lying on your back all stretched out is when your

tummy is at its flattest, and all your other front bits are also at their tautest. God knows what you must look like from the other side, but unless you're doing it on a glass table with a third party underneath it really isn't a consideration, and most likely if that is how you are doing it you are not the sort of person who would be self-conscious about your body, and are probably too busy entertaining top television hosts and politicians to be reading this book anyway.

Surveys the world over have revealed that body image is a major hang-up for women when it comes to having sex, and the wilier among us will, and have, come up with all sorts of ploys to keep the true nature of our form a secret from the one we so desire.

First, there's the old lights on/lights off debate. There is absolutely no point whatsoever in embarking on a session of sexual athletics in broad daylight or bright artificial lights if you really want to keep your stretch marks to yourself.

Mostly, complete darkness is your ultimate goal. OK, so this can be dangerous if you have to empty your bladder at some stage and need to grope your way to the door without spraining your ankle on his great clodhoppers along the way. Still, it's a small price to pay for maintaining the mystery of your shape.

I have a friend who believes that a single candle throws just the right amount of light on the subject, and by its very nature is automatically romantic as an added attraction. Never mind that it may set your bum on fire or torch your whole house! Any more than one candle, though, she warns, and you risk a shadow being thrown on your spare tyre or flabby arm.

This natural darkness is one reason why you should be more than usually sexually active on camping trips. Unfortunately, the fact that you are covered in mozzie bites, sleeping on rocks, suffocating in the 45° Celsius sauna that is your tent, and haven't actually spoken to your loved one since your first argument over which way up you hold the map — and that was when you first turned out of your driveway — usually rules this out altogether.

Stuff It!

There's also the old don't-no-matter-what-you-do-let-the-duvet-slip-off routine. This involves clutching on to the relevant corner of your bed linen no matter how much you are rolling or writhing or otherwise horizontal folk-dancing with your loved one of the moment.

I have another friend, not the same one as before, either, who took this skill to an all-time record-breaking high when she was caught doing the wild thing with a young stud by his soon-to-be-ex-girlfriend whom he hadn't quite got round to dropping just yet.

He did his best to stop the ex from coming into the bedroom when she arrived in the early hours of one particular morning, but to no avail. She was in no mood to be put off, and not only came storming in, but set about pulling the duvet off from the foot end of the bed. The new girlfriend, however, had a few years of expert duvet skills up her sleeve (had she been wearing one) thanks to a pot tummy she was eager to conceal, and clutched on for grim life to the top end of the duvet while pretending at the same time to be in a deep sleep. Despite the tug-of-love, the coma girlfriend remained completely covered from head-to-foot and went on to marry the object of her desire, so impressed was he by her grip and determination.

Once the duvet has served its purpose in keeping you completely covered, another common ploy is to make sure you are never seen properly naked in between being under it and in your clothes. This can be achieved in a number of ways — either by wrapping the bed linen around yourself as you sweep your clothes off the chair where you left them in a neat pile in the throes of passion the night before (yeah, right), or by whipping on the smelly old T-shirt he keeps under his pillow as he leans over to turn off the alarm clock. Of course, if you're really clever you will have positioned the chair close enough to the bed so that you can swipe your clothes off it and place the more alluring ones on underneath the duvet while he's in the bathroom.

Stuff It!

Another tip I have for feeling better about yourself in bed is to always make sure the person you are in there with is bigger than you, or at least of a similar size. If you can't get his jeans past your knees when you're secretly trying them on while he's getting the newspaper, forget it — you're looking at a lifetime of constantly comparing waist measurements. Also, who wants those skinny hip-bones digging into you and bruising your soft flesh while they're doing their business?

No, it's a great big hulk of a man you want if you are sensitive about these things. There's nothing worse than catching your bed-mate in the light of that second candle and realising he could get into the movies for half price. That's creepy. You really need at least 100 kilos of rolling blubber bobbing up and down on top of you before you can feel like Winona Ryder in the waif department.

Of course, there's always the option of losing the weight yourself and being smaller than your boyfriend that way, but it is a difficult method and one for which I never cared.

In a strange twist I have just been slumped in front of an episode of 'Sally Jessy Raphaël' in which weight-gain has ruined a couple's marriage via their sex life. Truthfully, it's not that much of a twist I am slumped in front of a talk show because I am, after all, addicted to them. Sally is my favourite because I want her to be my mother, but it's Oprah who always makes me cry. Nothing special, what with me being a blubberhead and all, but Oprah can even reduce me to crying at the abdominizer ads during the commercial breaks. Perhaps she's using subliminal shots of little defenceless animals being tortured or something, but whatever it is, she even had me sobbing my heart out the other day when she announced everyone in the audience had won a trip to Disney-world. It was so emotional.

Anyway, today I have been transfixed by 'I'm Desperate To Get Back With My Ex' in which David, 28, is trying to get back with Jessica, 25, who left him after he continuously rejected her sexual advances.

David shares with Sally Jessy and millions of complete strangers around the globe that he still loves Jessica very deeply and wants her back with all his heart, and that at the time he was rejecting her sexually he had put on a lot of weight and felt really bad about himself (sound familiar anyone?). He just plain got too fat to have sex. Then he went on a diet. Then she came back to him. Then he told her that her bosoms weren't big enough and could she please get some more, his treat.

Jessica, who's been standing backstage while the big lug has been pouring his heart out, is shaking her head and mouthing obscenities, especially over the bosomy bits.

When Sally Jessy brings her out to sit with her ex, we all know there's no hope for this relationship, even though David is skinny again and Jessica is a 36DD.

'If I wasn't such a lady I'd have come out here and kicked the living shit out of you,' Jessica explains in her best ladylike Bronx accent. 'David, it's dead, it's gone, it's over, it's past.' Just which part of that doesn't he understand?

Well, excuse me, but I'm not Sally Jessy — I can't pretend I care.

Cue mad, wild-eyed relationship adviser who tells David cryptically, 'You're not ever going to get big enough breasts,' and gives Jessica a hug.

Still, it's encouraging to know that men also have fat days when they want to remain untouched by human hand, even if David's breast augmentation fetish makes him a little out of the ordinary.

Can you imagine a New Zealand couple airing this kind of linen on national television?

'So Sharon-Tracey, what is it about Jayden-Hayden that made you try to cut him into tiny pieces and feed him to your axolotl?' the host, probably Susan Wood, would ask.

'Oh, nuthin' really.'

'But Hayden-Jayden, how did that make you feel?'

'Um, all right.'

'Tracey-Sharon, do you think he can ever find it in his heart to forgive you?'

'Yeah.'

'Is that true, er, Brayden?'

'Where's Lana Coc-Kroft? You said I'd meet Lana Coc-Kroft.'

I tell you, you'd be plenty dry-eyed for the abdominizer ads, wouldn't you? I've yet to succumb to the lure of buying one myself, so far, but that's only because I can't get my credit card out of my purse quickly enough.

What these things can't do for you hardly rates a mention! Why, I'm sure at least one promises to marry you, have your babies, a house in the country and a labrador dog. Five minutes a day and you have a washboard stomach the likes of which only your washboard has ever seen before. (Note to myself: must find out what a washboard is.)

I confess to spending just one morning in bed with the flu watching telly and thus becoming the proud owner of Victoria Jackson (whoever she is) makeup worth $250 which Ali McGraw told me would make me look young again, as demonstrated by Crystal Carrington's step daughter-in-law from 'Dynasty'. Oh, and I bought a special plastic contraption for doing step aerobics that came with a video on how to do it, but sadly the video and the step never seemed to be in the room at the same time so, um, would you like to buy it off me?

Getting back to the bedroom, though, I am one of the many who has employed the lighting/duvet/mysteriously-always-dressed methods of concealment with great success. But the best way around this whole problem is to not give a fig in the first place. It's hard when your thin girlfriends always find boyfriends much more easily (not to mention quickly) than you do, but especially as you get older, it's confidence that men are attracted to just as much as a tiny waist, long legs and a good set of bosoms. OK, maybe not quite as much but still, it's up there, unless, of course, the good set of bosoms is attached to long, blonde hair and then you may as well just get on the next bus to the convent and forget about the whole thing.

Then there are always the men who actually prefer the rolling curves and soft folds of a voluptuous woman. So, most of them you wouldn't cross the street to pee on, but they're still there, aren't they?

These days (and I'm not getting into any intimate details here for fear of my husband reading this part of the book and thus finding myself on the singles market again and having to practice what I preach) I'm practically a three-candle, no duvet, bugger your smelly T-shirt type who delights in competing with her loved one over who has the wobbliest belly and who can make it jiggle the longest once they've stopped jumping up and down. It's much better this way.

- 13 -
What's it all about, alfalfa?

*In which it is pointed out that the best way
not to eat a lot of something is to know just what it is
that you would normally eat a lot of — and then
generally try not to be near it*

IF I KNEW WHAT it was that made me eat more than it takes me to keep my body going I would be out there dressed in tiny ribbons of lycra, exposing my midriff like all the other thin girls.

Over the years I have time and time again examined and explored the reasons for never being able to understand the concept of moderation. Hell, I can barely spell it. I once went to a shrink. Twice actually. It was not long after I got back from living in England and I woke up and suddenly thought to myself, here I am back in Wellington, back in the same building I worked in before I left, back at the fat end of my wardrobe — what is the matter with me? When is anything going to change?

I found a psychologist in the Yellow Pages and went to see him as soon as I could get an appointment, using the fact that I was an urgent case to get my appointment bumped up, even though I had been struggling with my weight for 20 years or more, so this was not strictly true. His name was Mr Oberführer, or something very similar, and I'll tell you this for nothing — I needed a psychiatrist a whole lot more after I had been to him than I did before.

The first time I went to see him he wrote down everything I said in longhand! I could only get a tenth of my problems out in the hour I had. He was the slowest writer I have even seen in my entire life. At the end of our hour ($75 worth, do you mind) he said everything was my mother's fault, which I greeted with great skepticism but made another appointment anyway, as he'd really only had three minutes left at the end to talk to me and I thought perhaps he had left something important out.

Next time, he spent 55 minutes going over what he'd written down last time, which he seemed to have great difficulty reading, and then told me at the end everything was my father's fault. At this stage, I noticed he had the grand total of not one single certificate hanging anywhere in sight and I high-tailed it out of there, never to return.

I, personally, am not a great fan of blaming anything on anyone when it comes to eating too much. I know a lot of eating problems are caused by sexual or mental abuse as a child, and quite honestly, this leaves you feeling totally ripped off if you suffered from neither. Human nature makes us want to find a reason for irrational behaviour so we can deal with it in a formulaic way, but it's not always possible.

In the early days I hoped that my weight problem was caused by the fact that I was adopted, and I even confronted my father with this; once he'd stopped laughing, he asked how would I explain that I looked exactly the same as my non-adopted sister and had his legs? Actually, I'm still wondering about the legs.

I don't even really understand the concept of food as a comfort — it doesn't feel to me like I overeat because of a desire to fill some need. It truly feels like I eat to fill my stomach. Maybe I am a bit slow at recognising when I have achieved that feeling, and maybe there is a deep psychological reason for that, but with my history in therapy I am most unlikely to ever unlock whatever it is. Could the terrible truth just be that I like the taste of food more than I like wearing a size 12 dress? Apart from the sitting-on-the-end-of-your-bed-howling-with-misery-that-you-don't-even-fit-in-to-your-size-16 days, that is. That's when you want to wear a size 12 dress more than you want to eat, but you've probably already eaten. If you could remember that you like the taste of food more than wearing a size 12 every minute of every day your weight really would not be a problem.

I do suffer from the dreadful habit of treating myself with bad food when I think I truly deserve it. For example, if there's been a death in the family, the loss of a job, a bad period day, a bad hair day, a day ending in 'y', etc. Once you've given up that habit, let me tell you, you'll have no trouble with the fags, the booze, the coke, the crack, the wearing socks and sandals together.

Let me tell you about the foods I really struggle to eat in moderation.

Anything that falls into the category of nibbles. I love nuts and potato crisps, the saltier and oilier the better. Not for me your Slims and lo-fat jobs — just throw that spud in fat and fry the bejeezus out of it. I find it very difficult to be confronted with a bowl or, even worse, a packet, and not finish the lot.

Once when I was in Greece, trekking the 16 kilometre Somaria Gorge on the island of Crete with my friend Frances, we got into an argument over one of my favourite games: if you were stuck on a desert island and could only ever eat two things again, what would they be? (If you work in an office, try If You Had To Sleep With One Man In Your Department, Who Would It Be? That's fun, too.)

Frances chose garlic bread as one of her things but I refused to accept this, saying that garlic bread was more than one thing because it had butter and garlic as well as bread.

One of my things was salt and vinegar crisps. Frances argued that if her garlic bread couldn't be one thing neither could my salt and vinegar crisps because they were potatoes plus salt plus vinegar plus approximately one million additives and preservatives. I must say when I think about it now she was completely right, but at the time I simply could not see it and about 12 of those 16 kilometres were covered in total silence. Which just goes to show my great dedication to members of the crisp family.

So many times I have tried to cure myself of my addiction to crisps by buying huge packets and making myself eat the whole thing. Making myself? Yeah, right! Even I fell for that the first time, but after that I was just faking it.

I did manage to cure myself of a similar addiction to Milky Bar chocolate by eating a king size block at one sitting. I must say, this is not a very good way of getting out of the habit of eating food that is bad for you because it really only works for about two days after the incident and it's often likely that you would never have eaten that much of it over that period anyway.

I am a great fan of fish and chips, too, and I never just eat the fish and leave the batter. In fact, I have been known to do it the other way around. I am hoping I can blame my Catholic upbringing on my abiding love of this kind of takeaway because of the not eating meat on a Friday thing (shame about hot dogs); I think they abolished the meat thing anyway, the same way they got rid of Limbo where all the poor little unbaptised babies went, and St Christopher who was the patron saint of losing things or finding things or stealing things or eating meat on a Friday or whatever.

I could actually eat fish and chips for lunch, dinner and probably breakfast, too, if pushed. And there is nothing like a cold beer to wash them down with, either. Saints be praised, Christopher excepted of course, would there be a more fattening meal on the planet? Oh yes, fish and chips accompanied by white bread smothered in butter for the making of the perfect chip buttie, with extra salt! Sigh! Why am I talking about the saints? There is obviously no God in a world where all the most delicious meals are destined to make the movement of blood to your heart impossible, and to give you fat legs.

Stuff It!

The simple pie. There's another one. Boiled up bits of mutton cheeks and glue encased in flaky pastry — how can you go wrong? I am convinced a major reason I moved to Auckland was a subliminal desire to be near a gourmet pie shop in Ponsonby Road. Never a mince fan, probably because of the way it was served up in my younger years in a great boiled heap with peas, saved only by little triangles of pastry, the chicken pie is something I have difficulty bypassing. That, and bacon and egg. And lately steak and cheese. Combined with a milkshake, I would put money on the fact that it's one of the finest hangover cures in town.

Enduring (that's another way of saying 'You mean she's still alive?') Hollywood actress Joan Collins was recently in town, and while I did not go and listen to her politely refuse to dish the dirt on Linda Evans, I did get a blow by blow account of what she ate that evening, and it did not include the pastry surrounding her Beouf Wellington, but it did include the spuds, although other vegetables were only toyed with. She had about three spoonfuls of chocolate pud, and three glasses of wine. So going without pastry is probably what has left her in such great shape for a 73-year-old. I'm sorry, 63-year-old. Although I seem to remember some confusion about her actual birth date…

What famous people eat is always a matter of great interest to me. A couple of years ago I was back in London for a wedding, and my old friend Maggie was in town at the same time in between the European garden tours she was then conducting. I convinced her to come for lunch with me at San Lorenzo in London's posh Beauchamp Place. The glitteratti of London dined there constantly if the paparazzi pics I got across my desk at home at the *Weekly* were anything to go by, I told her. Princess Diana was practically on first name terms with the waiting staff, and didn't Jemima Goldsmith have her hen night there before she disappeared into the sunset of Lahore with Imran Khan. This place is so posh that credit cards and cheques are not accepted, only the folding stuff will do.

Maggie and I arrived and set upon the free breadsticks like rabid dogs. OK, I did. My eyes scanned the discreetly lit, cool as a cucumber surroundings for royalty, but to no avail. The best I could come up with was the actress who used to play Demelza in 'Poldark' who was sitting at the next table. We ordered entrées dripping in olive oil, and still Demelza was the best I could do. Then, just as we were finishing off our creamy pasta mains and wiping our plates with the extra bread we'd asked for, I saw her. Sitting three tables away from us was supermodel Elle McPherson, toying with a salad and inhaling mineral water at an alarming rate. So that's how she got that body!

I gave up all plans to order the cheeseboard, but sadly, cheese is another foodstuff around which I have great trouble practising moderation, especially when it is combined with Arnott's sesame crackers. Have you tasted them? If you haven't, don't. I grew up thinking that cheese was healthy because it came out of a cow, and it has been very hard for me to grapple more recently with its enormous fat content. And remember in the 80s, when every smart restaurant you ever went to was taking half a Camembert, crumbing it, deep-frying it and serving it with cranberry sauce? I was in heaven — and I thought it was a slimming appetiser. I absolutely adore those soft, creamy blue cheeses too. And the European Edams, Gruyères and the like. Even a Chesdale cheese slice or two has been known to slither down the gullet by way of a small snack. In fact, the only cheese I really don't like is that of the cottage variety, which would coincidentally be the only one it's really OK to eat, apart from ricotta, but I would rather suck the scum out of the plug hole in the bath through cheesecloth than eat that. The only thing I have ever discovered cottage cheese has going for it is that it helps stop the peanut butter from getting stuck to the roof of your mouth when combined with a sesame cracker.

Which brings to mind a small tale from inside of the Auckland radio studio where I once spent the hours between six and ten sandwiched between sports enthusiast Chuck E. Shearer and everybody's favourite TV presenter John (What? Me? Rig the votes?) Hawkesby, who jokes openly about how he has built a whole career out of recycling six clichés, although frankly, Chuck E. and I suspect it may only be four.

This particular morning we had mentioned on air the fact that had Karen Carpenter not died of anorexia she would have been celebrating her birthday. The microphone safely turned off, Mr Hawkesby laughed, 'I'd usually tell my joke here about how if Mama Cass and Karen Carpenter had shared the same ham sandwich, they'd both be alive today, but this year, I won't.' No sooner had he mentioned this than a light started blinking on the listeners' phone-line panel. Chuck E. picked it up. 'Wouldn't John normally be telling his Mama Cass and Karen Carpenter sharing the same sandwich joke about now?' came the inquiry.

When boxes of chocolates came flooding into the studio on Valentine's Day, John was surprised that I was giving them away almost before they reached my hot little hands.

'But you'd be having a whole chapter on chocolate, wouldn't you?' he asked. Well, I am actually happy to report that I have been blessed (believe me, when it comes to food, I'm counting these things) by not having a terribly sweet tooth. Honestly, with it, I'd probably be the most highly respected person in all of Tonga, if you get my drift, and you would. You wouldn't be able to miss it.

Most the time I can completely pass up chocolate or cakes, especially those dry cakes which stick to the roof of your mouth. I don't even go for chocolatey, caramelly slicey things. I like a bit of ginger crunch every now and then, but I'm convinced that it's only because I have a soft spot for gingers of the hair variety (Exhibit A, my husband). Don't get me wrong, should that box of chocolates be opened in front of me and left there, and the box be full of, say, dark chocolates, my hand would be reaching in with frightening regularity the same as the next lard-arse, but I try to build on my strengths and just steer clear of the stuff.

(I did as a 17-year-old try to impress a boy by eating 20 chocolate fish in one day, but I probably could have stopped at 15 if I'd tried. Actually, not so strangely, he chose my friend Frances-of-the-garlic-bread-is-only-one-thing fame to go out with instead of me.)

In the bakery I am more likely to veer straight towards the pies and sausage rolls — oh, sausage rolls, don't remind me! — but since my living on top of the bakery and discovering custard doughnuts phase I try not to frequent these places too much.

One of my oldest friends has a paunch of which he has long been very fond and a mother not afraid to speak her mind, which is, all of you with similar mothers will agree, a dangerous combination. This chap, in his 30s, worked for a pretty groovy company in Wellington and was out of the office one morning when his mother rang up to speak to him. 'I'm sorry, he's out getting pies for morning tea,' the helpful receptionist explained. 'What?' the poor wretch's mother shrieked into the phone. 'You let my son go to the bakery unsupervised?' We're still laughing.

One of my other major weaknesses is pasta. I swear I must have been Italian in my last life. If I wasn't a sausage roll, that is. I could eat pasta all day long, stopping only now and then to have fish and chips. On its own with butter and pepper. With great galloping dollops of pesto. With bacon and tomato and basil. With those expensive pottles of ready-made sauce from the supermarket. With just about anything.

I am not much of a cook. In fact, I have had the good sense to marry someone who is, so I am now the setting the table and clearing the plates person. However, it is wicked of me to share this recipe with you, but this is exactly the sort of thing you should not eat.

Stuff It!

Bad For You But Easy To Make Smoked Salmon Pasta

Garlic
Onion
Red pepper
Olive oil
Salt and pepper
Mushrooms
Smoked salmon (either offcuts or slices)
Lite sour cream (Ha! As if there really is such a thing)
Capers
White wine
Pasta (dried Italian is the best)

Put the water on for the pasta and while you're waiting for it to boil, finely chop the garlic, onion, and red pepper, and roughly chop the mushrooms. Put the pasta on to cook. Meanwhile, heat the oil in a deep frying pan, add the garlic and onion, and cook till the onion is transparent. Add the pepper and mushrooms, and cook until mushrooms are piping hot. Establish this point by constantly popping them in your mouth until you finally have to spit one out. If the mixture seems dry add white wine to moisten it; add more if you like lots of wine in your cooking. Add smoked salmon. It will fall apart somewhat so don't worry about cutting it into nice little slices. Finally, add the lite sour cream and capers; stir over medium heat until hot, using the tasting method as described before. Put cooked pasta on a large platter or in a large bowl and mix in smoked salmon mixture. Serve with parmesan cheese, green salad and hot french bread. Ideal for feeding lots of people when you haven't much time or inclination for cooking.

Would you like me to share the recipe for the only pudding I know too? OK.

Stuff It!

Absolutely Disgusting Chocolate Chip Cookie Fat Fest

1 or 2 packets of chocolate chip cookies
Bowl (yes, bowl) of sherry
Lashings of whipped cream with a dash of vanilla essence
Cadbury's Chocolate Flake bar
Glacé cherries
Almond flakes

Dip chocolate chip cookies in the sherry and place in a ring on a flat tray or platter. Smother with whipped cream. Place another layer of sherry-laden cookies on top and again, smother with whipped cream. Continue doing this until you have about four or five layers, then smother the whole lot in cream, including the sides, and put it in the fridge, ideally overnight. Next day, sprinkle the flake on top of the chocolate chip and cream ring, along with glacé cherries and almond flakes. Cut wedges of it, and eat and eat and eat. The chocolate chips stay crunchy but the sherry-soaked cookie goes squishy like a cake. NB, I once got confused and made this with brandy instead of sherry. It took one and a half hip flasks and made you cry if you got too close to it.

Now, do you believe me when I say this is not a diet book? My recipe for not eating any of the aforementioned foods is to make sure I am never in the same place as them, unsupervised (yes, it's true, mothers are always right). For low-fat alternatives to the above, go immediately to another galaxy and call me if you find anything.

– 14 –
How eating at restaurants can be bad for you

In which it appears that cholesterol is not the only thing that might get you after a night out on the tiles

THERE'S SOMETHING ABOUT ordering food off a menu and knowing you will not have to tidy the kitchen that can get a person hooked on eating out. Restaurants also tend to be places where laughter is the first course and hysteria (the good kind) is the dessert. (If I start talking about the tonic of the mountains about now, please see that I am institutionalised.)

Quite often it is not the food that draws a diner to a particular eatery, but the company. I've only ever been attracted by the food, myself, but does that come as a surprise?

I have had some of the best and worst moments of my life in restaurants. Of course, it is not possible to have a completely bad moment in a restaurant because even if you are being dumped by your boyfriend, discovering you have only three months to live and finding out that after a lifetime of thinking you were a brunette you are actually a ginger, you are in the presence of food, and that in itself is a good thing.

Some of my happiest memories involve sitting around plates of food cooked by a complete stranger in the company of my friends. I remember a delicious dinner eaten with a friend at a place called Roscoff's in Belfast; a birthday surprise at the French Horn in the English countryside only mildly ruined by me falling off my chair laughing at a joke being told by someone at the next table, on whom I was eavesdropping; a wonderful lunch at a Waiheke Island vineyard just last summer.

At one stage of my life I became addicted to the Sugar Club in Wellington where chef Peter Gordon cooked a fillet of beef with pesto sauce atop a bed of shredded beetroot which I swear melted in your mouth. I'm glad to say that months of pouring my hard-earned cash into this eating emporium made no sense at all, but when I read recently that Peter Gordon is now chef at the Sugar Club in London and that Madonna got turned away three times because she hadn't made a booking, I felt a bit better. Don't ask me why, I'm still trying to work it out myself.

I remember the day I wagged school and went to a flash restaurant with the man I couldn't impress by eating twenty chocolate fish, and flicked my butterball onto the neighbouring table. In a strange twist it's the last time we ate out together without the order being shouted through the window of his car, and given the mess a butterball can make on a silk tie, I'm frankly not surprised.

Given my propensity to snap my ankles I suppose I should be grateful that when I slipped down some steps at a London eatery after celebrating a flatmate's birthday I only broke my bum. 'And it already had a crack in it,' my sister roared with laughter and I don't blame her — I'd always thought that people who had alleged to have fractured their tailbones were foxing in the interest of a few days off work myself. But I can assure you that having a broken coccyx is no laughing matter. After two days of lying in the bath trying to relieve the agony but wrinkling myself to sharpei proportions, I finally took enough painkillers to get a taxi to the Osteopath Training Clinic where I had been told the fees were half price.

What I hadn't been told is that at the training clinic osteopaths moved in packs of one tutor and five pupils, and this was not something that I learned until I was on my hands and knees with no pants on and the six-pack was examining my bruises. What I really wanted was for a crack to open up and me to disappear down it, but it seemed to me at that particular point in time the world already had an extra open crack.

I realise that it's hard to go from that mental picture right back to a three course meal, but let's just remember that the injury was sustained at an eatery, making it yet another memorable dining experience.

Speaking of which, my husband once made the great mistake of confessing to me that as a child of maybe seven years old, he had gone to a greasy spoon in Wellington's Courtenay Place with his family, ordered two bits of fish and chips, but had only been able to eat one of the bits of fish. To this day, he confided, especially in moments of hunger, he still thought about that piece of fish and wished he'd eaten it.

He has since learned not to arm me with such ammunition because as a result I will taunt and jeer him for years, in the nicest possible way, of course. The funny thing is that now I think about that piece of fish too. I wish he had eaten it.

Actually, twice in my life I have been physically assaulted in restaurants by complete strangers, which I am pretty sure is either quite unusual or a sign that I spend far too much time in restaurants.

The first time, I had just returned to Wellington after living in Sydney, and was walking down Willis St in Wellington with a friend after the movies one night when I spied a welcoming-looking eatery called the Armadillo.

We went in and asked for coffee, which elicited a very strange response from the man in charge, whom I later found out was known around town as Pete The Meat. He snorted with derision and said, 'Come on now, you should know better than that!' which I let slip because I thought I must have misheard it. Pretty much the best thing I could think of to do at this stage was to sit down at a table for two near the door. The moment I sat down, Pete the Meat came tearing towards me and emptied the contents of my bag on to the table while shouting gibberish at the top of his lungs. Then, and this is the part I really hated, he pulled my hair. Naturally, everybody had stopped eating and was looking instead at the spectacle unfolding before their very eyes.

'Come on, Annie,' laughed Pete the Meat hilariously. 'You know better than to come in here at this hour of the night asking for just a cup of coffee.' Aha, I thought, as the penny dropped.

'You're going to be terribly embarrassed,' I told him, stretching my neck to keep my ponytail going in the direction in which he was pulling it, thereby lessening the pain. 'I am not who you think I am, I am her sister.' The hair-pulling continued, as he derided me for trying such a pathetic scam.

'We look very much alike but I have just got back from living in Sydney,' I squeaked, as my scalp started lifting from my skull.

'Good one, Annie, yep, I've never heard that one before,' he taunted.

'I have never been in here before in my life,' I wailed, 'plus I am two years older than her. My driver's licence is lying underneath that chair over there. Look! See it.' You could have heard the penny that earlier dropped, drop.

'This is not a joke,' I told him, and looked into his eyes, which was considerably painful due to the whereabouts of my hair at the time. At that point he realised the error of his ways, but from the look of him, there was no going back.

'Oh, you kidder,' he spat half-heartedly, releasing my ponytail with an extra tug, and with that he disappeared into the kitchen never to be seen again. I pulled my ponytail around to its original position, collected the contents of my bag and went home.

'He called me Annie?' my sister Anna raged when I unfolded the tale the next day. 'I'd have whacked him in the head just for that.' That night, we dressed in identical clothes and went together to the Armadillo. As we walked in the door, Pete the Meat came shooting out of the swinging doors from the kitchen. He looked at us, went back into the kitchen, came out and looked at us again, then went back into the kitchen. He never spoke to either of us ever again.

The second time I was assaulted was partly my own fault because I got up from a table full of my friends at an Italian restaurant in Auckland and walked over to what I assumed was the toilets. However, by the time I opened the door and went inside it became perfectly obvious that it was in fact where they kept their spare jars of pickled vegetables and everyone's coats, and what the hell was I doing in here? I stood there for a few seconds, already suffused with embarrassment, and then opened the door and sat down at the closest table.

'I have just completely humiliated myself and I desperately need you to engross me in conversation,' I told the people sitting there, and thanks to the litres of red wine they had already consumed, they obliged. Their names were Bill and George and Something Else, and by the way they were knocking back the vino they were in advertising. When my face had returned to its regular colour I tried to excuse myself to return to my own table, but my new friends would hear nothing of it. 'No, no, you must stay,' they cried. 'No, no, I must go,' I whimpered repeatedly, until I caught my husband's eye on the other side of the room and he picked up my bag, said our goodbyes to our real friends and came to rescue me.

'Really, I must go. See, even my husband says so,' I insisted, slowly standing up.

'No, no,' said Bill, the burlier among them, grabbing my arm, 'we insist.'

'No, no,' I countered, pulling myself away from him, 'I insist.'
For a split second he released his grip and I headed at speed for
the door. Unfortunately, my other half, who was perhaps not
quite aware of the seriousness of the situation, was not so quick.
By now, Bill was on his feet, gripping for dear life to one of my
husband's arms, while I had the other. We pulled and tugged and
pulled and tugged in a most ridiculous fashion until I had the
good sense to yell out, 'Look, over there, isn't that the new boss
at Saatchis?' at which the ad man's concentration faltered, and we
legged it to the car and sped home.

In contrast, I met one of my best friends in a restaurant where
he was doing a stint as a maitre d'. Such was his deep sarcasm and
evil wit I was attracted to him over the first bellini, and by 3 a.m.
I was dancing on the bar with him, juggling lemons and throwing
lilies around the room like a two-bit stripper. It was a truly
memorable occasion and one we have relived many times at a
similar hour throughout the years in various eateries, but
thankfully we are now too old and cranky to stay up past nine
o'clock at night and have just as many laughs over a nice hot cup
of tea, best drink of the day.

- 15 -
Truly, madly, weekly

*In which a horrible nightmare becomes a dream
come true, even though we all know
there is no such thing*

ONE DAY A NICE MAN rang me up and told me I was the editor of
the *New Zealand Woman's Weekly*.

This was quite a coincidence because I had been having a series
of dreams in which I went and talked to a nice man about that
very thing, then came home and wet my pants laughing before
going to the loo, only to be bitten on the bum by a boa constrictor wearing Bruce Forsythe's toupee.

In the most recent dream I'd had, which had definite nightmare
potential, I went to a flash restaurant to have lunch with the man
who owned the company, but instead of charming him with my
witty repartee and revolutionary thinking I became obsessed with
my bad ordering skills.

In a last minute rush I ordered the seafood chowder and the
sushi. Well, excuse me, but had I left my brain at home in my
other handbag? Yes, because this seafood chowder came with all
its shells still attached, and I was a messy eater at the best of
times! Worse than that, being nervous always makes me hungry.
Actually, I have yet to experience an emotion that doesn't.
Needless to say, by the end of that chowder, I was splattered from

bosom to bosom (in the absence of cleavage, this is quite a distance).

Luckily, the owner of the company was very nice and seemed not to notice, but then I did have a large chunk of mussel beard stuck between my two front teeth which may have made it difficult for him to concentrate on my chest.

When the sushi arrived, it came on a little platform — with chopsticks, two complications on which I hadn't banked. Despite all my efforts to wrangle the raw fish and riceballs directly into my mouth, a nori roll lost control and bounced off its platform and towards the owner of the company. In a flurry of ninja skills the likes of which I had never attempted before, I arrested its progress with my chopstsicks and devoured it without once taking my eyes off the top of my dining companion's head.

Then I went to the lav and hyperventilated for a while.

Actually, now I come to think of it, those weren't dreams — that really did happen! Apart from the boa constrictor wearing the 'Generation Game' rug, that is. That really was a dream.

Anyway, very soon a letter came confirming my appointment, and eventually I realised it must be true because after hours of rigorous testing a team of scientists I had hired for this purpose confirmed it did seem to have been sent to me at my address.

Frankly, I had my doubts about their authenticity as they said their results were completely dependent on my providing twenty-two bottles of mescal tequila and a box of lemons but, nevertheless, I went into my bosses at the TV station where I was working as a lowly researcher and resigned.

'I've got good news and I've got bad news,' I said.

'I'm sorry and you are…?' they enquired. I reminded them a couple of times, but their expressions remained blank so I threw in a couple of other people's names instead.

'OK, give us the bad news first,' they said, in an obvious attempt to hurry up whoever I was.

'The bad news is I quit!' I said. 'The good news is I'm the editor of the *New Zealand Woman's Weekly* now!'

This of course, left me with only the one career prospect of actually being the editor of the *New Zealand Woman's Weekly*, which turned out to be quite a lot harder than just talking about it and clinking congratulatory champagne flutes with my friends.

Things didn't exactly get off to a great start when the nice man invited me in to meet the staff, who seemed as bewildered by my appointment as I was. I told the nice man that nibbles and drinks were essential as I didn't feel comfortable anywhere without them but even less so with people whose jobs rested in my somewhat clammy hands. He agreed wholeheartedly that it would be a much more relaxed affair if a bit of wine and cheese was thrown in.

I turned up on the appointed evening to find a large room devoid of any comestibles but full of nervous-looking employees who'd been asked to line up to meet me. I went around one by one and shook each hand just like the Queen does then turned around at the end to gaze upon them in their entirety as the drinks trolley was wheeled in. It was not to be. It appeared that as I shook each hand its owner then went home and, frankly, without the lure of a cocktail or two I did not blame them, in fact, I pretty much wanted to go home myself. The drinks trolley was a no-show.

The first few months at the *Weekly* went by in a whir. In fact, for the first week I was actually under the impression that the *Woman's Weekly* was a tractor parts reference guide for the wives' division of Federated Farmers. Luckily, someone put me right pretty early on in the piece.

I was still convinced at this stage that the real editor of the magazine was going to open my door one day and expose me for the fraud I truly was. I'd never been in charge of so many people before! I couldn't remember their names. I couldn't ask them to wear name badges. I wanted them all to like me.

The first week I was so busy trying to get my head around why all the things that needed doing needed doing and when, that I never even went to the loo during the day.

The second week, a severe coffee drinking attack combined with a feeling that wetting my pants in front of my new team would not add to my credibility prompted me to use the loos for the first time.

Everything went very smoothly until I tried to get back into the office — but there was a lock on the door and a keypad. Nobody had told me the number! What to do? What to do? Start banging and shouting in the hope someone would hear me? Wait until someone else's bladder filled up and they were forced out here as well? Keep standing here with a face red as a beetroot, and the awfulness of it all drilling a hole in my spleen? I went back into the loos to kill time and lo, there was another lady washing her hands at the basin.

'I'm terribly sorry to interrupt,' I said, ' you wouldn't happen to know the code to get into the *Woman's Weekly* by any chance, would you?'

She stopped washing her hands and looked at me.

'Of course I know it, Sarah-Kate. I work there.'

Embarrassment upon embarrassment — I had failed to recognise a member of my own staff. Maybe now would be a good time for the real editor to show up? Did this ever happen to Ita Buttrose?

One of the conditions that the publisher had talked to me about before offering me the *Woman's Weekly* job was fronting the magazine's television commercials. It had been my original plan during the interview to suggest Joanna Lumley for the job, as she did such a good job of playing an alleged fashion editor in the top-rating TV show 'Absolutely Fabulous'. What a hoot it would be having someone who couldn't even remember where her office was and got stuck on the back of a toyboy's motorbike wearing no knickers telling everyone to buy the latest *Woman's Weekly*!

However, as the interview progressed it became clear that the publisher thought the new editor should do this job, and because I was a crawly bum-licker, I agreed, and possibly even made it sound as though not only had it been my idea in the first place, but that it was my definition of fun, fun, fun!

Of course, little could be further from the truth, and anyone who has avoided having their photo taken for ten years because they're sick of being reminded how much bigger than everyone else they are will back me up on this one.

Naturally, once I had accepted the job and the ads became a reality, I panicked.

'Everyone will think I'm fat,' I wailed at home to my long-suffering husband, who at least had the good sense not to point out that it's hardly a fact I could conceal with any great success.

It suddenly occurred to me that the thing I hated most about myself and had battled with for as long as I could remember was going to be splashed across national television for a period of many months. Do you think I worried that people would think I was a young and inexperienced editor who was toying with the country's best-read magazine? Not for a second. I was worried they would think I was fat, and I couldn't think of any way to disguise it.

This business of not wanting people to know you are fat is not peculiar to me either, although I know that to those who haven't ever been very overweight it will sound ridiculous.

But, for example, once I was trying to convince a friend of mine at work to come to the company weight-watching group with me, but she was proving very unwilling.

'I'm just not ready for everyone here to know that I have a weight problem,' she said, at which we both pissed ourselves laughing and headed off to the caff for fish and chips. But I knew exactly what she meant. I myself had gone for years without ever once mentioning my weight to some of my closest friends. Obviously I couldn't hide the fact that everything I wore was on an elastic waistband, but neither was the issue out in the open as a problem. They thought I didn't care. I didn't want them to know that I did.

Now I was going to be coming into peoples' living rooms in the *Weekly* ads sending out an XOS, and I didn't like it one iota.

For a start, the *Weekly's* advertising agency and I had completely different ideas on how I should look. They thought I should look like a magazine editor and I thought I should look like me, and it's a battle I wish to this day I had fought harder, because I lost it.

My fabulous idea for keeping from television viewers the true story of my bulk was to wear black; the agency guys told me I would look like a witch and no one wore black on television if they wanted to appear friendly.

I explained that I had always worn black, that it was my signature, that I felt comfortable in it, it suited me, it flattered me, I wanted it, could I please, please, please have it — go on, please?

The agency guys said they had been in the business 25 years and knew what would work. I think the agency guys were probably very good at going out to lunch.

Despite my great discomfort at what I was wearing, the filming of the first commercial went quite well because the agency guys seemed surprised that I wasn't freaking out in front of the camera, even though I had told them I played Winnie the Pooh in the school play.

In the ads, I had a young male assistant called Jeremy who I would either eye up in a lascivious manner or put down in a 'hilarious' fashion. When I actually saw the first ad on TV, which was an eyeing up job, I just about had a heart attack. For a start, I looked about 75 years old, but worse, I looked fat. I know this should not have come as a surprise, but it did. I took to my bed with a box of tissues and some salt and vinegar crisps and cried my head off.

Incidentally, throughout the campaign, the *Weekly* was hounded by phone calls from lusty young wenches trying to get hold of Jeremy. Some claimed to have gone to school with him. Some claimed to be closely related to him. Some claimed to be trying to get in touch with him to turn over huge fortunes he had been left by recently deceased relatives. Unfortunately, none claimed he was a model called Khan who didn't actually work at the *Weekly* which was, of course, the truth.

The second ad I quite liked because I was allowed to wear my own white linen shirt and Jeremy and I got to tootle around the harbour together in a funny little boat.

By the filming of the fourth or fifth ads, I was having serious creative differences with the agency guys, and without the charm and diplomacy of the director I probably would have taken our entire collection of Rachel Hunter pictures, which as you can imagine was quite substantial, and shoved it up their jacksies.

By the seventh ad, wearing a shade of rose even a corpse would not normally be seen dead in, I was spending an hour locked in the loos sobbing on the make-up artist's shoulder, begging her not to make me go out and continue filming. The scripts for the ads were often written as we went on funny-shaped scraps of paper, and in my opinion not only fell well below what I would consider humourous but didn't even seem to be highlighting the stories most likely to sell a magazine.

That, combined with my inability to smile in the right degree of wryness and my misery at being incarcerated in rose synthetic, had all the ingredients of a living nightmare.

Oh, where was Joanna Lumley when you needed her?

Thankfully, the ads were only a very small part of my job at the *Weekly* and most the time I was too flat-tack with the gruelling schedule of just getting a magazine out to worry about how my size was going down, so to speak.

I had decided early on never to run fad diets in the magazine because after years of trying them, I knew they were mostly rubbish and that the only way to really shift the pounds was to eat less and exercise more. OK, I said I knew it, I didn't say I practised it.

The other decision I made was to steer away from the wafer-thin models of the time. This actually proved quite hard, and the fashion editor was often left tearing her hair out on shoot days when an agency had promised to send along a curvy size 12 and instead a stick insect would walk through the door, slicing through her clothes with her hip bones as she moved. Well, we were the only ones asking for extra meat on those waifs, I suppose.

This move, although it was only tiny, struck a chord with many readers, who wrote in to say that it was about time we stopped pretending that all women were cardboard cutouts and got real about our size, but many felt I stopped too short of the real truth. After all, what's the difference between a size 10 and a size 12? They had a point, but then again I didn't want the *Weekly* to be seen exclusively as a fat women's magazine because I also had letters from quite a few petites begging me to stop banging on about the roly-polies and give the skinny-minnies a look in. Strangely, my sympathy for them was not as forthcoming. When you have nearly a million readers every week, it's quite hard to keep them all pleased, I find.

I have to be honest, too, and confess that while I wanted to make a bit of a difference to how people thought through the pages of the magazine, I didn't personally want to become a spokesperson or role model for the over-16s, and it was already getting to the stage where I was being approached by other media on the fat issue and being inundated with voluminous knickers from large lingerie companies.

And before you start thinking I just wasn't prepared to put my tummy where my mouth was, the whole point I was trying to make was that being a size 16 or over should not be a big deal; it shouldn't mean you have to wear a completely different style of clothes from anyone else; it shouldn't mean you need a special spokesperson or role model; it shouldn't mean anything.

It certainly shouldn't mean that you find yourself being described one day in a tedious monthly magazine as looking like the 'Coopers & Lybrand tower on red nose day' accompanied by a private joke in which you claimed to 'never accept an invitation unless it's involves a three-course meal'. What a laugh! Why, I haven't enjoyed a jibe so much since that spotty funeral director's son called me Fatty in the playground. What a wag! What a wit! Whatever happened to him? Now he's married to a fatty? Oh dear.

Oh well, I was sick of being a lard-arse anyway. Once I turned 33, the thought of turning 34, 35, 36, 37, 38, 39 and eventually 40 and still crying at the end of my bed because I had nothing to wear held little appeal.

It was time to get me to a fat farm.

- 16 -
It's not called a camp for nothing, you know

*In which the kilos are scared off with a local,
hi-energy torture treatment, used only
in the wilds of Australia*

MY BIG QUANDARY in the plane on the way over to Camp Eden in Queensland's Currumbin Valley was should I be making the most of my last access to unsavoury foodstuffs or should I be getting in the swing of things already? Sheer fear of being weighed at the end of my journey eventually prompted my refusal of the chicken-or-fish and little bottles of chardonnay, but not before I'd bolted down two packets of peanuts — well, how could they show up on the scales?

I was met in Brisbane by a luxury limo which rolled me smoothly toward the rabbit food haven. Was I tempted to jump out of the moving vehicle at Surfer's Paradise and spend the next two weeks holed up in Jupiter's Casino playing pokies and ordering room service? Hell, yes! But good sense prevailed — that and the fact I couldn't work out how to open the door from the inside.

Real, unmitigated panic hit, however, as we approached the locked gates of the military-style enclosure nestled at the foot of the rainforests in the Currumbin Valley just north of the Queensland-New South Wales border. Those gates meant business. There'd be no getting over those in the dead of night — the strongest knicker elastic notwithstanding. I half expected to see Corporal Shultz (a slimmed down version, obviously) standing inside the gates insisting, 'I know nussing, I know nussing,' as bulge-battlers begged him for details of the nearest fast-food emporium.

The limo rolled up to the first building at the foot of the hill and unloaded me. The pain was about to begin. There was no going back — despite offering to give the limo driver my first-born child if he took me with him. Despite offering the opportunity for him to father that first-born, right now, in the back seat. Tyres squealed and he was gone.

I straightened my shoulders and entered the building for registration. To my horror, other people lurking around the office seemed to be quite a regular shape. I had imagined that my corpulence would go hardly noticed at a fat farm, for goodness' sake. Isn't that partly why I was here? To feel smaller than other people, if just for two weeks? No such luck, campers. I had struck a thin week. Sigh.

At this stage it was pointed out to me that while the gymnasium, swimming pool, playing fields, tennis courts and bush walks were all at the bottom of the hill, our beds and, more importantly, the dining room, were at the top. Sigh again.

Still, registration over, I was instructed to cross to the gymnasium where I would be weighed and measured, then it was up to my assigned room to check out my roommates. No single rooms here unless you were prepared to pay big time, and then you may as well be sitting in the Sydney Hilton with a mai tai in one hand and Matt Dillon in the other, wouldn't you say?

But back at the gym I was sweating big time over the weigh-in. In my experience there is only one thing a person who battles the bulge hates more than people who can eat and eat and eat and not gain weight, and that is being weighed. Ever since that fleeting moment when I weighed 9 st 2 in 1981 I have avoided scales like the plague, and I know I am not alone in this. For the first few years I would eye them up in other people's bathrooms, torture myself for a while, and then leap on them, but the ensuing fright and horror was so great and the results so very, very far away from 9 st 2 that I eventually gave up altogether. Until I got to Camp Eden.

All I can say is that you could nearly double that weigh-in figure from 15 years before. This was deeply upsetting, because now my corpulence had a number attached to it and the number was very high, and at this stage I felt very bad and had to dash off for a cry in the lav. I don't care what anyone says, denial can be a wonderful thing. Still, I suppose the best place to feel deeply depressed about the weight that has risen up and taken over your body is at a health farm on the first day of a two-week stay.

Once I'd recovered from the shock of my own weight my fitness was tested and revealed to be Below Average, which was actually good news at this stage. Well, it could have been Poor or Very Poor! So all those years of sometimes going to the gym had finally paid off, eh.

Mildly cheered up (OK, I was desperate) I started up the hill, because it had not escaped my notice that it was lunch time. But in a strange and horrible twist, the fact that I now knew how much I weighed made me feel much fatter than I had when I first came through those Stalag 13 doors. Now where's the sense in that? It's like feeling a million dollars all day then trying on a pair of size 14 jeans in a shop and not being able to get the zip up. All of a sudden you're ten pounds of shit in a five pound bag, and yet you're still the exact same person that first walked into the shop. I hate that.

Anyway, I dragged myself up the hill in the 40° heat (this is probably much more fun when you have a big gap between your thighs as opposed to the alternative, if you know what I'm saying) and girded my loins to meet my roommates.

Now I have never been particularly comfortable in the company of strangers. I once went to Spain on my own for a month to experience the joys of meeting other like-minded travellers en masse but went home after the first week, having talked to less than one other human being.

So I was uneasy about sharing a room with three others. However, I needed to visit the room in order to change my sweaty clothes for lunch, and lunch was not something I was going to miss out on. As it turns out, I needn't have worried. I had just two roomies; one of them was a very loveable, enthusiastic lawyer called Felicity, and the other a deeply skeptical working mum, Natalie, both from Sydney. My only concern was that by the look of them they were both Above Average fitness and probably hadn't collapsed in a fit of the vapours after finding out how much they weighed because a) it wasn't that much, and b) they already knew. Still, Natalie and myself hit it off immediately and headed for the dining room.

I have heard people return from Camp Eden saying how much they loved the food, but I was not one of them. Never a huge fan of vegetables, I was not impressed to see that the table was laden with every salad you could possibly imagine and nary a drip of mayonnaise in sight. Plus, there was a special person stationed at one end to make sure you only got one wafer-thin slice of bread. Despite the sweltering temperature I opted for the hot soup because it had large things floating in it. I eyed up the special person to see if they could easily be overwhelmed in a fist fight but decided against it, what with it being my first day and all and the whole point of being here involving the loss of weight.

The rest of the day could be spent playing water polo, volleyball or going for bush walks, none of which thrilled me in the slightest so, as they were all optional, I retired to our cabin and my trashy novel. (Well, at least there was no rule against bringing trashy novels in — you couldn't bring in magazines or newspapers, radios, gin or cigarettes. In fact, on arrival at Brisbane airport one of the customs dogs went ballistic at my suitcase and I got dragged off to the side and quizzed about the contents.

'Are you sure there is no food in that bag?' the uniformed officer wanted to know.

'Well if there is I want it sniffed out now,' I replied. 'I'm going to a health farm, for goodness' sake.'

As it turns out, all we could find was my hiking boots with a slight trace of mud on them because a certain husband hadn't cleaned them properly, although the officer was convinced that my bag had at some stage in the very recent past been used for carrying oranges or had at least leaned up against some oranges. Some specific dog, huh?)

It wasn't just sheer laziness and the exhaustion of being catapulted out of the denial of what I weighed that had me taking to my bed in such a way, I must point out. I had a bruised spine as the result of falling off my horse the week before and I was throwing back the painkillers like they were going out of style. Happily, the narrow, hard beds seemed to suit my aching back quite well, and with the help of Penny Vincenzi I was soon transported away from this place.

The whirr of a helicopter brought me back down to earth with a thud. I had heard from one of the staff that it would be carrying another New Zealander, Kendall, a real character, they assured me, who owned an island just off Auckland and was possibly the loudest person ever to visit Camp Eden. What joy.

Kendall was a barrel of a man in his 40s with stocky legs and fingers dripping in gold. The island he owned turned out to be Waiheke (well, *he* never said he owned it) and forget Camp Eden, he was possibly the loudest man on earth. Elusive about the details of his work, rumours flushed through the camp that he was a modern-day hitman, especially after one dinner time conversation in which the gist seemed to be that he had 'bashed the snot' out of some hapless victim who required hospital attention as a result.

Stuff It!

Kendall spent the first day making lewd and leery comments to every woman in sight, and if you were very special he would honour you with a wedgie, which means he'd pull your togs up so hard they'd get wedged in your bum. Now, as someone who has spent much of her life picking her pants out of her bum (I know I'm not special in this regard) this held very little appeal, but Kendall steered clear of me anyway.

After a dinner of many different vegetables, Natalie and I retired to our rooms where we character-assassinated other people in our group, especially Kendall. This became a pattern for the week. Really, it was just like being at home!

At 5.30 the next morning the gong sounded. Allegedly it was time for tai chi outside on the grass knoll between the cabins, although as we all know, it was actually time for still being in bed asleep.

Tai chi began and ended with everyone standing in a circle massaging the person in front of them. This started off with a few choppy motions around the neck, but to my horror ended up with your buttocks being squeezed and pummelled by the person behind you. Naturally, this was Kendall's favourite time of the day and the owner of the buttocks in front of him would normally be squealing in pain within seconds, but at least it stopped him from pinging her bra strap. At one stage he managed to lift someone off the ground by their underpants.

Imagine that before quarter to six in the morning! Frankly, I find it hard to balance on two feet at that time of the morning let alone just one, especially while my arms are whirling around my head and my eyes are crossed as I simulate Flamingo Sees Old Boyfriend Through Thick Spectacles, or whatever.

For the uninitiated, tai chi is a gentle collection of exercises based on stories to help you remember the movements. Snow Maiden Collects Lotus Leaves, Sprinkles Them On the Ground and that sort of thing. Our tai chi instructor was a gorgeous, tanned bombshell who is, incidentally the sister of Tineke Bouchier, Selwyn Toogood's former 'It's In The Bag' sidekick. A more serene person you'd be lucky to find and she stood in front of us on the dewy grass as the rainforest slowly awoke around us. 'Jack Rabbit Digs The Garden, Knackers All Your Carrots,' roared Kendall. The mood was broken.

Anyway, another round of karate chops and it was time for the Brisk Morning Walk, or BMW, a winding track through the bush, on which you were timed. Once more I was reminded that I was the fattest person there. Can you believe it? The fattest person at the fat farm? Surely this was some cruel joke. What was wrong with all these people? I had spent the first day anticipating the arrival of the bus load of cheese and deep-fry fanciers from Doodlypipply that would take the heat off me in the weigh-in stakes, but it was not to be. They were no doubt holed up at Jupiter's, eating their own bodyweights in chicken-in-a-basket, and I was hoisting the fat flag on the BMW alone. With this highly motivating thought reverberating in my head I took off. OK, so everyone was thinner than me, but there were a couple who were older than me, one by 30-odd years, I'll get her on the BMW if that's the last thing I do, I vowed. Unfortunately, the last thing is what I did. Yeez, they breed them strong out here, but.

God, what was I doing here? I railed. I could stay at home and have my self-esteem torpedoed for free, thank you very much, and eat meat.

Thankfully, though, the BMW was followed by breakfast — the highlight of the day as far as I was concerned. You chose from a selection of delicious fresh fruit or a wet, cold porridgey thing which I loved because it filled you up, and I still have it for breakfast every day. (For those of you keen to try this gastronomic delight, the recipe appears on page 156.)

After that it was down to the gym for either a stretch class or yoga, at which Kendall would keep about three — sometimes only two — people in fits of laughter with his running commentary on people's bums and bosoms and their general suitability to be *Playboy* centrefolds.

Stuff It!

At nine it was time for people who were on their first visit to Camp Eden to adjourn upstairs for The Circle. Now friends of mine who had been to Camp Eden before me had remained strangely mum on this part of the programme. How many of you will immediately snap the book shut if I say 'group therapy'? Yes, well that's probably why nobody bothered to mention it to me, either. And for someone as preoccupied as I was with not looking like a dick in front of other people, The Circle started out as sheer torture. Luckily, my skeptical roommate Natalie and I could roll eyes at each other across the room while we were writing nice things about other people on their backs or dancing around the room to Madonna in broad daylight.

When we got to the part where everyone had to say why they were at Camp Eden I was amazed (but given the fat count, obviously, relieved) to find out I was the only one there just to lose weight. Some of the younger, more gorgeous ones were there because they'd been dumped by their boyfriends (I can only imagine it had never happened to them before); some were stressed-out business people; some were struggling with things that were holding them back — abusive parents and the like; some were searching for their faith; some had suffered a terrible loss. Why I felt positively shallow saying I simply wanted to shift a few pounds! OK, quite a few, but just pounds nonetheless. I was practically lucky.

In all there were 16 of us and I won't bore you with the details but by the end of the week Natalie and I were jumping around making dicks of ourselves just as happily as everyone else, because the whole point really was that it doesn't matter what anyone thinks of you, it's what you think of you that counts. The definite highlight was having to stand in a circle of these people on the last day and have each one compliment you out loud. While sometimes the group had seemed overcrowded until that point, gladly I would have doubled, nay tripled, the size of it at that moment! It was music to the ears of someone who had been publicly compared by a total stranger to one of Auckland's biggest buildings. 'I love your eyes,' said one of the group. 'I think you have an amazing voice,' said another, (obviously not the person who stood next to me for the singalongs). 'You've got gorgeous dimples,' and not of the thigh variety either. 'You really make me laugh.' Now wouldn't 16 people telling you how wonderful you are turn a fat and ugly day around in a hurry?

Anyway, the daily routine was to pour out of The Circle at noon and trudge up the hill to lunch — aka more salad. Tea or coffee was not on the menu by the way, and no matter what anyone says, I was not the first to spit out the dandelion substitute and scrub my tongue in disgust. OK, so no one quite had my reach, so sue me, that stuff was poison. There followed an hour of free time until reassembly down the hill at the gym. At this point, a roster had gone up telling you what your personal schedule was for the afternoon and it might go something like this:

2 p.m. Water Aerobics;

3 p.m. Massage;

4 p.m. Bush Walk;

5 p.m. Volleyball.

No points for guessing that the 3 o'clock appointment would be my favourite.

Getting over my loathing of team sports was certainly an issue that needed addressing *tout de suite*, but not for the first time I thought to myself, 'Well, I'm here. I can't escape. I have noted all the exits and they are all guarded. I have told too many people I am coming here. I have to get on with it.' Which led me to believe that back in the real world I was not inclined to just get on with things but rather to avoid them from the outset or do them under duress after an awful lot of whingeing, which, don't get me wrong, is an excellent system, but perhaps like most things you like should be done in moderation.

Well, imagine my surprise when I enjoyed the team water sports. And that's wearing togs and everything! How many other things were there that I've always thought I hated but, in fact, don't, I wondered? Well, there's artichoke hearts for one but, no, I do actually hate them.

Needless to say, by 6 o'clock deep exhaustion combined with extreme sweatiness had set in with a vengeance, and it was once more up the hill to clean up and get changed for the hundredth time for dinner, which was definitely an improvement on lunch, and on a Wednesday we even had fish! Special treat! Roll out the barrel, let's have a barrel of radishes and lima beans with a lemon juice dressing. Yay!

Wednesday, in fact, was a very bad day in two respects. Firstly, I was plain too scared to go on the flying fox that careered down a steep hill towards certain death; my certain death anyway, although everybody else survived it. This made me feel like a prize patsy, especially as I suspected it wasn't only my fear of heights that was holding me back — it was my fear of everybody seeing my fat bum strapped into the world's most unflattering harness contraption, and that was pretty much anti everything that was being drummed into me at the point.

The second thing was even worse.

I started developing a soft spot for Kendall.

Call me completely mad, but there is something about being stuck in an enclosed Australian rainforest with a bawdy sexist pig and without any deep-fried food that simply twists a girl's viewpoint.

'I could tell you thought I was an arsehole,' Kendall confessed to me over sprouts that night. 'But frankly I didn't like the look of you, either.'

By Thursday morning it was my neck being clobbered by Kendall's ham fists and my buttocks being squeezed, clunky gold rings clinking, with great verve. He then announced himself my personal trainer and vowed to increase my speed on the BMW so I would no more be humiliated by coming last every morning. This he did by running along behind me, slapping my bum and yelling, 'Get going, you prize heifer, or I'll bash the snot out of you, too.' Which humiliation was worse I couldn't figure out, but by the end of the week I had shaved four minutes off my time so if that's what I was after, I guess I got it.

At the end of the week I was gifted with the Kendall In Yer Face Award for Perseverance which myself and my pummelled buttocks richly deserved.

I did not exactly cry when Kendall left, of course, but I was undergoing something of a terrible internal struggle at the time because Natalie was attempting to lure me away from the prison grounds with the promise of crisp chardonnays and all you can eat steaks up the coast at Noosa. Why didn't I forget my second week of health and fitness and embark on a proper holiday with her and her husband?

It was a pretty good question, actually. Why didn't I? Well, for a start, the first week had been too much like hard work to go completely to waste. But more importantly, I think I had simply reached the point where I knew if I didn't do something about it now, my weight would become even more of a millstone around my neck, literally and figuratively. This was more than two weeks of torture at a health farm, it was the beginning of the rest of my life (small break for extravagant song and dance number).

The second week zipped along as I bowed to routine, jumping out of bed at 5.30 and sprinkling the lotus leaves with great calm. It was definitely a more dignified routine without Kendall but not quite as much fun, although something in the food had affected most people's bowels and the gentle awakening of the forest was hampered by the renting of splendid farts and the air was rich with flatulence.

My new roommate was a woman in her 50s from west Sydney whom I took to the moment she came back from her first Camp Eden meal exclaiming, 'They call that muck food, well, it's bloody disgusting.' According to her, there wasn't one member of the staff who would not benefit from a gigantic steak and a slurp of red wine, and next time she came she was going to leave behind all her pants suits (she had brought quite a few) and instead load her bag with crackers and cheese and some chocolate to get her round the BMW. And some prunes because, oooh, her bowels were giving her gyp and over her dead body was she taking any of that herbal sawdust they were handing out to other constipatees.

Second Wednesday around, I conquered the flying fox, but mercy me what a palaver. Like most things I'm scared of, it had weighed heavily on my mind (yeah, like I needed extra weight) and become a Big Deal because I knew I should do it but I really didn't want to. A bit like being editor of the *New Zealand Woman's Weekly*, really.

I peered down the flying fox's steep trajectory every morning as I passed it on the BMW. Would I do it this week? I didn't want to. But would I regret it if I didn't? Would it bug me all Thursday and Friday if I didn't have the guts to give it a go and would I think about it in years to come as the Thing That Bugged Me All Thursday And Friday?

By Wednesday I was in an absolute lather of indecision. With the rest of the campers I gathered at the top of the hill and started the process of watching everybody else wheeeee down the flying fox while I ran the exhausting rope relay involved in pulling the harness back to the top of the hill after each downward flight. How dare all those skinny little things jump so happily off the platform into nothingness and whizz through the air with such glee. I couldn't possibly do that myself. What if the harness broke? What if the whole thing collapsed? Sure, there were some hefty flying foxers jumping off before me (Week Two wasn't as thin and pathetic as Week One), but their bums didn't look as big as mine. What if? What if? What if?

Finally, sick of being a nancy, and more importantly sick of the rope relay, I ventured towards the platform. It's no secret that I blub easily and this moment was no exception. Gingerly I was led to the edge of the cliff, clipped on to the harness and counselled.

'It's the stepping off that's the hardest bit,' the fox monitors said kindly, which made me cry even harder.

'You're clipped to the tree,' they said. 'You don't have to jump until you're ready.' The tears were squitting out the side of my head like a cartoon character.

'Imagine the tree's whatever you're afraid of,' they said. 'You can leave it behind if you want to.' I was sobbing like a child — what was the matter with me? Was it just the threat of ending up a large splat at the bottom of the hill or was it something else?

'Don't be scared,' they said. 'Take the leap.'

Take the leap? Don't be scared? I teetered on the brink of that cliff and thought about how I'd let a few extra pounds hold me back in my life. Why was I scared of what other people thought of me? Why did I judge my own success on how other people judged it? Who were these other people anyway? Why did I let them bother me when I could be big as a barn and the people I knew and cared about would still love me and they're the ones that count?

Take the leap.

Don't be scared.

I took the leap.

Like they said, stepping off into nothing was the hard part. Within a nanosecond I was whizzing down the hill at enormous speed, my arms and legs akimbo, shouting at the top of my lungs, as free as a bird, my fear and loathing left at the top of the hill still clipped to that stupid tree. The journey lasted about nine seconds. I had spent ten minutes on the teetering platform, crying and being cajoled into jumping off. Now, I felt fantastic. I bounced back up the hill to join the rest of the campers feeling like I weighed about nine stone.

'Do you realise,' someone whispered as they hugged me when I got to the top, 'there wasn't a dry eye up here when you jumped?'

– 17 –
And you thought being at the fat farm was hard?

In which in an annoying your-mother-told-you-this-twenty-years-ago-but-you-thought-you-knew-better-way, you mother turns out to have known better

AS IT TURNS OUT, being at a health farm was the easy part. That was torture, but at least it only lasted for two weeks. It was when I got home that the real hard work started. I knew that to make any sense of what had been drilled in to me and pummelled out of me over the past fortnight, I had to change my whole lifestyle, not just the contents of my fridge.

Of course, I felt like a million dollars when I got home because I was 5 kilos lighter than when I left, and I have always found that it is easier to lose weight when you have already lost some. I know that sounds obvious, but there really is a certain natural high to finding your elasticated waistbands are becoming looser on you, especially when you suspect that over the preceding months you have stretched them to their maximum capacity. It feels good to know that you can lose weight, even if it's only a drop in the bucket. If you are lucky, you can even feel like you are on the beginning of a rather exciting journey. If you are unlucky, you can just feel hungry.

It was very helpful that everybody commented on how well I looked. I could see for myself that my face was not so puffy, my eyes a more sparkly shade of green, their whites, whiter (What am I? A soap commercial?) I felt relaxed. I felt happy. I felt in control.

I am loathe to say this because it is the sort of thing that makes me spit with rage when I hear other people say it, but it is true. The weight fell off me. All I was doing was cutting out fat and quadrupling my exercise, and it was coming off in chunks.

At least four mornings a week I would get up early and go for a walk before work. I'd plug in my Walkman, slap on a baseball cap and get moving down the street and around the block and as far as I could go in the hour I set aside. Soon it was only taking 55 minutes to cover the same distance, then 50, then 45, then five. OK, for the last one I was getting a taxi, but you get my drift.

Actually, one morning I was walking through the Domain in Auckland on my circuit and as I rounded the bend past the winter tea gardens I saw a gaggle of geese lurking underneath a tree at the side of the road. How quaint, I thought, as I strode towards them. How like Marlon Brando and his henchmen in the *Wild Bunch* I thought, as I got closer. From a distance they had seemed fluffy and cute. Up close, they looked stooped shouldered and menacing, and for a moment I fancied they were wearing black leather jackets and matching caps. I gave them a swerve as I passed them but despite that, Marlon started waddling towards me, giving me the hairy eyeball all the way. In an effort to frighten him off I stamped my foot. Big mistake. Within the blink of an eye he and his evil cohorts stampeded me, making the most frightening racket you've ever heard. Suddenly, having your bazookas massaged by a mental hospital escapee seemed like fun. These birds were out to get me. Marlon started biting (or whatever it is geese do) my leg, and in an instinctive fight for survival I kicked him in the head. It only enraged him. But he caught my second bootful in the chest and as quickly as he had turned on me, he and his pals turned away. 'Watch out for the geese,' I yelled at a jogger coming my way. 'They're in attack mode.' He looked at me as though I was some kind of deranged breast squeezer, and when I turned and looked behind me there was nary a goose in sight. I am sure I saw Alfred Hitchcock step behind a tree.

Needless to say, after that little confrontation with the animal kingdom, I varied my route.

When I wasn't fighting off flocks of angry bird life, I would get up at 5.30 a.m. and drive the half hour west of Auckland to where I kept my horse, Treasure, to ride her and exercise us both. In the winter this was particularly hazardous because it would be pitch black and the only way I could ever tell which horse was mine was by calling her name as I stumbled down the race towards her paddock. The one horse that ran away from me would be her.

I have to tell you a story about Treasure, actually, because it's another one of those it-could-only-happen-to-me stories that helps make me the complete and utter doofus that I really am.

I was actually supposed to go to Camp Eden a week earlier than I did but two nights before I was due to fly to Queensland, I went riding in the forest with my friend Nicky. It was a beautiful summer's evening but Treasure, who is only a young horse and a bit excitable, was playing up, shying at every blade of grass that blew in the wind and trying to bolt on me at the drop of a hat. Finally, after she narrowly missed firing me at a very pointy looking tree in a bit of the forest we call the Dead Wood (probably because so many people have fallen off their horses, been spiked by pointy trees and died there), I gave her a healthy whack with a whip, which I had borrowed as I didn't usually carry one. Little did I know it was Treasure's day for not being whacked by whips of any description but especially borrowed ones. She simply reeled around and careered off the beaten track at speed, heading into a thick clump of trees. I wobbled around on top of her in an entirely useless fashion until the low branch of a member of the forest family did us all a favour and got rid of me. Next thing I knew I was lying on the ground groaning and feeling as though my bum had been pushed up to the top of my head internally. This is not a good feeling.

Once I had gotten over groaning and being winded and was trying to suck my bum back down to its rightful spot, I tried to stand up, but my back was hurting so much I could barely breathe. Nicky raced off on her horse to get help, while I was left lying in the middle of nowhere wishing I was dead already. Treasure got sick of this pretty quickly and ran away. Loyalty is not her strength.

After what seemed like a very long time, Nicky came back with Liz, who owned the farm where our horses were kept, and as I was going nowhere under my own steam, an ambulance was called.

At this stage Nicky was standing up so the ambulance could see where it needed to come to, I was lying face down in the dirt, and Liz was sitting next to me. Next thing there was a screech of tyres coming to a halt on the gravel road and the sound of many doors opening and much excited chatter.

I twisted my head around and there appeared to be three middle-aged ladies dressed in brightly coloured vests who identified themselves as the New Muriwai First Aid Emergency Team or similar. Either I had concussion or there was a definite touch of the Judean People's Front about them. Or is that People's Front of Judea? My point exactly.

I knew I was in trouble when one of them asked Liz if she was OK.

'It's not me that's hurt,' said Liz, 'it's her,' pointing at me, although I would have thought it plain that my lying on the ground with my face in the dirt crying might have led them to think, in the first place, that perhaps I was the injured party.

Stuff It!

'Do you know,' I heard one of them say, 'I was so excited when the bleeper went off I could feel the adrenaline pumping.'

'Well,' said another, 'I was so excited I put my socks on but I forgot my shoes!' A casual glance at her feet, which were after all the part of her that was closest to me, revealed this, sadly, to be true.

At this stage, I was given an oxygen mask, although I was in no need of oxygen and it kept falling off my face and scratching my nose. Then, just when I thought it had got farcical enough, a small altercation broke out over whether I was 'alert and cooperative' or 'alert and unco-operative'. This was because at the time of the accident I was in the process of moving house and was genuinely trying to establish which address was the more appropriate one to give them. This was misdiagnosed as some form of concussion or obstreperousness and I'm not sure which condition they eventually settled on but I hope the one with no shoes on wasn't in charge of the forms.

Finally the ambulance arrived and I was loaded in, which excited the first aiders greatly, and caused them to clutter around the open back doors, yelling, 'Is she on the machine? Is she on the machine?' That was the last I ever saw of them, but Nicky tells me the final chapter unfolded as they only narrowly escaped being run over by the ambulance as it left the scene. I am truly and eternally grateful to them for providing some humour at a difficult time.

Of course, I was deeply embarrassed at the difficulty the ambulancemen seemed to have in lifting me anywhere, and their cheerful reminders that, 'no offence, but I was no feather,' made me hurt even more than I already did. Why, it's almost worth going through the whole rigmarole all over again now that I am 20 kilos lighter — but I want shoes on every foot this time around.

My trip to Camp Eden was put back a week, a week which I spent on my back unable to move, apart from to put deep-fried foods and takeaways into my mouth. Well, in for a penny — in for a pound!

Stuff It!

Once back from my two weeks on Fantasy Island, though, I settled into a routine of coming back from my walk or morning ride, having my Camp Eden breakfast and then heading off to work as usual. Lunch would normally be pita bread and hummus with tomatoes or avocado or something similar, or a salad if I was going out, and not a Cesar Salad either because it turns out they're not as slimming as you would think, although that shouldn't really come as a surprise because they're a bit too yummy to be good for you.

Then I'd come home, maybe have another bit of pita bread to stop me eating my own fingers, and wait for my husband to come home and cook me a lo-fat or no-fat dinner, usually with chicken because it is of fowl that I had dreamed during my two weeks as a vegetarian.

If pushed, I would even make dinner myself, but it would never taste as good as his would. Well, that's my story and I'm sticking to it. And wouldn't you, too?

Alcohol was another hurdle. Once back in the comfort of my own home, I tried to limit myself to three glasses of wine a week. I said I tried. I didn't say I always succeeded.

In fact, sometimes I failed spectacularly. For example, there was the night in Wellington just after I had announced I was leaving the *Weekly* when I found myself lying on my back in the foyer of Wellington's posh Park Royal hotel right next to the sign that said, Caution! Slippery Floor! at 3 o'clock in the morning. My friend Susanah was laughing so hard she seemed incapable of helping me, and such was the level of my overindulgence when we got to the seventh floor I had to re-enact the whole slapstick disaster once more outside the lifts.

We had been out for dinner and consumed much more wine than was necessary, and I had managed to single-handedly pick up a whole table of insurance brokers who were so boring they were even forced to comment on it themselves.

After my side-splittingly hilarious (not) re-enactment, I ran to my hotel room, threw open the door and told my ever-patient and sensible husband who'd been in bed for hours (sense a pattern here?) that I had a lovely new boyfriend. Then I dropped all my clothes to the floor, looked in the mirror and screamed, 'Somebody's put a baggy, fat suit on me. Get it off!'

Incidents like those, I am happy to report, are the exception rather than the rule. The thing I find about a few drinks is not so much that they make you feel like eating a big meal at night, but that they make you feel like eating 47 meat pies the next day, and that's ruining two days instead of just one.

However, I have to admit that while I am trying very hard not to be a fatty boom-stickers I do need a life, and being of Irish extraction, I do like a bit of a knees-up. Hence, I try to drink alcohol only once a week. And for those of you who have seen me hijacking the karaoke machine at an Auckland nightclub in the wee smalls, that was my one night, OK?

- 18 -
Helpful hints from someone having a fat day

*How to get your butt moving when it mainly feels
like lying in front of the video machine*

I AM HAVING such a fat day I just want to go to bed and wake up
when it's tomorrow.

Sometimes you have them because you snuck in a high-fat
takeaway the day before and followed it up with half a black
forest Moritz icecream, and sometimes you have them for
absolutely no reason at all.

A friend of mine who is no stranger to womanly wiles — in fact,
he's probably in the *Guinness Book of Records* somewhere —
dropped around recently to take me out for a drink and just as
we were about to go out, I stopped and said, 'I think I might just
feel too fat to go out today.'

He rolled his eyes and whinged, 'Why do women always say
that?' This cheered me up enormously because most of the
women he's gone out with have waists the size of my arm and it

always helps to know other people feel just as shitty some days as you do, especially if they are stick figures.

At the moment, I deserve to feel floofy because I have done absolutely no exercise in two weeks due to falling over in humiliating circumstances and spraining my ankle.

We had spent the weekend with friends at Waiheke Island where I had conquered my fear of making a fool of myself trying a water sport by making a fool of myself trying a water sport.

I've so far steered clear of anything which requires flailing your thighs around in a flubbery fashion, but that is just what is involved in getting on a Sea Doo, some kind of giant jet ski, or at least, it is the way I do it. Heavens, I'm surprised Greenpeace didn't show up to give me a push — they usually do.

I screamed with terror as my fearless husband rode the waves, and then when he finally insisted I had a turn at the controls, I shot straight out towards Australia while he yelled in my ear, 'Turn, turn, turn', like a deranged New Seeker.

Such was my embarrassment that I was forced to turn on a group of small children playing too near me on the beach afterwards. 'If I wanted children this close I would have had some of my own,' I snapped at them. 'Please go and play somewhere where I can't hear you.' They smiled happily and moved in an annoying we-love-it-when-we-rile-the-big-people way, which infuriated me even further.

Still shaken from all that excitement we caught the 6 o'clock ferry back to Auckland on Sunday evening, along with hundreds (or was it thousands?) of other weekenders, most of whom were behind me when I spectacularly twisted my ankle in front of the ferry terminal and collapsed, face down, into the traffic.

My two bags and the hat I was carrying disappeared into the oncoming traffic and people and, worst of all, as I lay there paralysed I felt an eerie breeze up my back and knew, just knew, that my dress was up where it ought not be and my pants were exposed to the world. Big knickers may be practical but you could never really call them sexy, could you?— never mind that *Vogue* magazine says they're back in.

Anyhow, for some strange reason my husband, although standing, also seemed paralysed, and another man scraped me up off the ground and helped me hobble back to the footpath. By this time, my other half had come to his senses and I was able to lash out at him with my good arm, berating him for leaving me in a pile on the road. Tears poured down my face, much more to do with the exposure of my bum than anything else, although my ankle was giving me gyp and already looked like it had swallowed a tennis ball. The people standing behind us felt so sorry for me they gave us a ride home! Yay for not paying the taxi fare.

That was two weeks ago and the darn thing is still all swollen up and giving me grief. I am particularly protective of my ankles them being, as I have already explained, the only naturally thin part of my body, which may explain why they have a habit of snapping on me.

Remember Sweetwaters, the 80s rock festival? Yeah, well you weren't there then. The second year Sweetwaters exploded onto the rural pastureland of the Waikato, I was just popping back from elevenses at a friend's tent when I jumped off an eight-wire fence and heard a nasty crack that seemed to come from my ankle area. Sure enough, my ankle was rendered incapable of holding up the rest of my body. I sat there by the fence for about two hours until somebody felt sorry enough for me to get their boyfriend to take me to the hospital tent on the back of their motorcycle. You bet that was a helluva ride! At the tent they told me I'd fractured my ankle and gave me two disprin. That night I hobbled up to the main stage with the help of a small divining rod crutch broken off a tree and a yobbo who then proceeded to try to feel me up at every opportunity, and me disabled!

Next day I went to Middlemore hospital and got plastered and then had to fly home in a plane where much to my friend Julie's amusement I was pushed through the airport in a wheelchair by my very own air hostess and taken out onto the tarmac where a forklift, do you mind, lifted me up onto the other side of the plane to what everybody else was getting on. At the other end of the journey, another forklift was there to pick me up, despite my insistence that I could crawl down the stairs and over to the terminal unaided. This time, the forklift kept me up in the air and drove me across the tarmac while the ground crew wet themselves laughing.

Six months later I broke the same ankle skiing at Whakapapa on Mt Ruapehu. As you can imagine, I am a thoroughly meritless skier and it was only my rush to get finished for the day and get home that had me going so darn quickly down the Waterfall run. Forty-four somersaults later I was left lying in a heap of broken sunglasses, poles, skis and that same old ankle. This time I had to wait until the ski patrol could find me, then they packed me into a big yellow banana and skied me down the hill to the chairlift where two burly men lifted me on board.

'Too many Weetbix for breakfast this morning!' one of them chirped, and he wasn't talking about himself either. If I hadn't been strapped in so tight I could barely breathe I would have boxed his ears.

Getting the ski boot off my shattered bone was nothing compared to the torture of driving home via the hospital in Taupo. My flatmate, Helen, had to drive my beaten up old Triumph Herald, which was bad for two reasons. One because she hadn't brought her glasses with her — and I cannot stress how heavily she relied on them for seeing — and the other because she had only got her licence that week on her second go after crashing the car on her first. Doomed, doomed, I was doomed. Luckily a six-pack of Steinlager helped ease the pain.

Until this latest sprain I have looked after my lower pins pretty well, but now I am holding them completely responsible for the blobbiness which has enveloped me. I've just had to go and put my jeans on again to prove that I can, and I must say they are feeling a little firm around the waist.

To be honest, I had much more trouble with the exercise thing once I started my new job as a breakfast radio host, which involved getting up at 4.30 in the morning. I had my little routine down pat when I did a nine to five job, but once I started getting up so early I found it harder to build it into my day as a regular feature, since I seemed to spend quite a lot of time working out when I could go to sleep again.

The key is to get exercise over and done with as soon as possible (I think you will find Oprah agrees with me on this one) for the simple reason that this relieves you of the duty of having to make up excuses not to exercise later on in the day.

One little trick I have is to disguise exercise as something else altogether. My favourite one is disguising it as going to the movies. This has got to be good for you. There's a big cinema complex about 25 minutes' walk from my house, and often in the afternoons I will walk to the movies and walk back again. The success of this method depends entirely on your ability to not buy popcorn, of course, but if you feel bad about not purchasing anything at the Nibble Nook, get one of those little bottles of water for 63 times the price it'll cost you in the supermarket.

The only flaw with this scheme is that sometimes the combination of being up early, walking down there and being in a big, dark, room proves too much for me, and I sleep through the whole thing. I have slept through movies like *Independence Day*, *Die Hard 3*, *Michael Collins* and a slurry of others, although the bigger explosions usually wake me up.

If I'm having trouble fitting exercise into my life — which I do — I will try to walk over to a friend's house for dinner instead of driving, keeping a constant lookout for marauding breast squeezers all the while because I have a spooky feeling that chapter of my life is not over.

Walking to the shops is always a good idea, too, because if there is anything that can motivate a girl it's the zip-zap of the credit card going through the machine in exchange for a completely useless piece of crap that she will never, ever, use. I have a whole cupboard full of these things, but I am happy in the knowledge that I have often walked up hill and down dale (what is a dale, anyway?) to get them.

The other thing I have trained myself out of is the deep-rooted desire to get the closest humanly possible parking space to the place I am going to. Do you do that? I must have wasted at least a whole year of my life if I add up all the time I have gone around the block, waited, gone around the block again, psyched the old age pensioner out of getting in to the park before me, lost, gone around the block again, waited, parked in the handicap park, got out of the car, seen someone with a walking stick, got back in, gone around the block again, etc., etc. Now I deliberately park further away just to get my big, old butt up and moving, even if it's just for five minutes, because for me the desire to be sitting very still doing nothing comes very naturally and it's a habit I truly want to break. I even once heard some expert say on the radio that you could lose weight by getting up and changing the channels on the TV rather than using the remote, but I can't see that ever catching on.

On days when I feel like wearing lycra, which are few and far between, I will go to the gym. I have found one not far from my house where it is perfectly OK to wear holey old singlets and not smell very nice. Finding the right gym is the absolute key to being able to exercise in one. For years I have belonged to a big, inner city gym that practically requires me to seek an hour of therapy before I can step in the door. There are women in this gym whose entire exercise outfits are made of less fabric than my sweatband — and I'm talking about the one around my wrist. These women wear make up and have fancy hairdos. These women are already thin — for the life of me I can't figure out why thin people need to go the the gym so much. These women have the instant effect of making me feel like a sad and lonely 'before' in a room full of 'afters', and this is not a feeling conducive to exercising. Especially when it has taken me half an hour to find an illegal park for the car that is possibly being towed aways as I bounce, and the instructor is 12 years old and so slight I keep getting her confused with the cord that opens the window.

My first exercise in any aerobics class is always to swivel my head around and scan the room looking for somebody — anybody, please, anybody — fatter than me. Often this person does not exist or has stayed at home eating pink buns that day. This will leave me feeling depressed before the warm-up.

At one of these step aerobic classes the instructor actually laughed when the third person in a row fell off their step and practically had to be hospitalised. I found myself burning off more calories at having a heart full of hatred for the gym than I was losing in the exercises themselves.

For a while, I fought the system and made a nuisance of myself at the suggestion box, but after I had voiced my concerns to three different people at various levels of inferiority, I decided it was more satisfactory to cram the box full of anonymous obscenities and see if the police could ever track me down; then I had an absolute brainwave and stopped going altogether.

In a strange and sad little twist, although I have done just three aerobics classes at that particular gym in the past year, and although I have been thoroughly Camp Edened, I still pay my monthly membership *just in case*. Just in case of what, you may well ask. I'm asking it, so why wouldn't you?

Meanwhile, at the scuzzy gym around the corner from my house I am on a series of 10-trip tickets that are costing me a fortune. My routine now is to cycle for 20 minutes, walk on the running machine for 20 minutes, and then spend a final 10 minutes on the stepper machine, which is so incredibly hard and horrible I can't believe it's not as good for you as the other two machines but apparently it isn't, so why bother.

Once I tried to use the abdominizer but I somehow got my

Stuff It!

head stuck in it and had to cry out for help.

I am a very unfriendly person at the gym and my preferred modus operandi is to have my Walkman on from the minute I start till the minute I finish. I have made up a tape that I use for walking or exercising which contains music the likes of which any self-respecting grown woman would be ashamed to admit. Suffice to say Wham!, Madonna and Take That feature prominently. I strongly advise that if you need extra motivation you get a boppy tape to listen to.

I toyed with my system once and played a different, slower tape, but found that I couldn't cycle or walk as far as I did with the more uplifting (yes, well, George Michael is uplifting to me) music. It made absolutely no difference on the stairmaster of course, because nothing can help you on the stairmaster, short of a severe heart attack followed by a lengthy recuperation in a faraway sanatorium.

I have absolutely no doubt in my mind whatsoever — and in fact I have tried time and time again to disprove this theory and even attempted once to forget it completely, to no avail — that exercise is the key to losing weight and keeping it off.

Not only does it speed up your sluggish metabolism and help you burn off fat more efficiently, but it makes you feel smug because for once you've actually gotten off your chuff and gone out there and done it, leaving your endorphins reeling in shock and partying on down in your bloodstream.

The trick is integrating exercise into a life that revolves pretty much around lying in front of the TV, reading and eating.

They say that when exercise becomes as natural a part of your life as any of those things, you're on your way down the scales.

But then they also say that there is such a thing as lo-fat sour cream, and we all know that is simply not true.

- 19 -
Make fat your friend, then drop it

In which helpful hints are expounded, but heed this warning — they will only work if you try them

I CAN'T PRETEND that I don't still dream about fish and chips (although the one where Brad Pitt rubs them all over me is welcome any day) and white chocolate Magnum ice creams. I don't still eat them, but I dream about them. OK, I've had one of each over the past year, but it wasn't on the same day or nothin'!

Most days, I try to steer clear of the fatty foods that will test my willpower because it is easier for me that way, and if I go out, I try to pick the lowest-fat thing on the menu, unless it has anything to do with tofu, in which case you can forget about it.

At home, I find the biggest help is to always have the right kind of food in the house. This generally involves yelling down the phone at my husband to stop at the supermarket on the way home from work, but on the odd occasion I do have to go out and actually do the dirty work myself.

I always go big on the bulky fruit and vegetables first, because if you are naturally mean with your money like me you don't like the trolley getting too full because it means you are spending too much money; by putting the large-volume healthy foods in first, you stop filling the trolley sooner. This will only make sense to women and even then only unhinged ones, like me.

(By the way, I have been testing an interesting hypothesis lately at the supermarket. Never mind adding up every last cent on a calculator. Did you know that you can pretty much calculate that every supermarket bag is going to cost you around $20? True story. Try it for yourself.)

I have other tips that I employ to keep me on the straight and narrow, including that old chestnut about never going shopping on an empty stomach because it's like rinsing the sink out with coffee — or something or other.

I do not go down the potato chip and other savoury snack aisle. Certain mayhem reigns downs this track. I do not go down the biscuit and chocolate delicacies aisle. I may never return.

I go straight to the feta and cottage (so help me God) cheese without stopping for the Edam, Gouda, Camembert, Brie, Cambrazola (exquisite!), blue debresse, etc. Get the picture?

I do go down the magazine aisle where I read all the good bits of the magazines and then put them back without buying them in the exact same way that used to infuriate me to the point of reaching out and slapping innocent strangers when I was editor of the *New Zealand Woman's Weekly*. Come to think of it, that's my favourite part of shopping now!

I buy chicken breasts or thighs without the skin, because even though it's a bit more expensive, I know if the skin is on there I will be tempted to leave it on because we all know that actually that is the best part.

I always buy something relatively healthy that I can eat the minute I get home, otherwise I find myself dawdling at the deli dreaming of a snack I can eat in the car on the way home like that chicken samosa or that scotch egg or that other thing deep-fried in crumbly bits and covered in sour cream. This is where havoc can truly be wreaked.

Stuff It!

Instead of any of those completely delicious things, I buy some ready-made hummus and a packet of pita bread. Amazingly, a piece of the latter, bunged in the microwave for 40 seconds and used to scoop up the former, fills the hole with alacrity and isn't too bad for you as long as you don't overdo it on the hummus.

If you are like me, you want instant gratification and if instant gratification is lying in your freezer, fridge or secret jar that nobody else knows about, then that's what you'll dip into. But if carrots and apples are all that you can get your mitts on, that's what you'll settle for. It's a queer old world but the best we have to be getting on with, as Brendan Behan (the late literary lard-arse) used to say.

As I mentioned, ever since my two weeks of strict vegetarianism at Camp Eden, and that's over a year ago now, I have craved chicken. Every time my husband asks me what I want for tea, my answer is, 'chicken dinner'. Hell, even when I ask myself that question the answer is the same. I am even prepared to share with you two of my favourite chicken dinners so you too can savour their delights and forget forever the sausage wrapped in thick, buttered bread (I'm sorry, you'd only just forgotten it?). You need a really good, non-stick frying pan for both of these meals, the deeper the better.

Warm Chicken Salad

Potatoes
Golden kumara
Pumpkin
Broccoli
Chunky, dried Italian pasta such as penne
Tomatoes
Avocado
Red pepper
Spring onions
Garlic

Stuff It!

Mushrooms
Chicken thighs or breasts, skinned and boned
Lemon juice

Chop potatoes, kumara, pumpkin and any other vegetables languishing at the bottom of the fridge for that matter, into chunky, bite-sized pieces, and bake on a tray in the oven with a tiny bit of canola oil, some lemon juice and sea salt, until they are crunchy on the outside and squishy on the inside, if that's the way you like them. This usually takes an annoyingly long time, like 40 minutes. Get the pasta going so it will be cooked and ready by the time you've done all the other bits. Chop the chicken up into bite-sized bits and sear it in the frying pan with garlic (optional), adding lemon juice for moisture. I like to cook it quickly on a high temperature. To establish when the chicken is ready, cut one piece in half and if it is cooked through, pop it in your mouth. Mmm! Take time to enjoy! Throw the mushrooms in the frying pan and cook them too. Steam the broccoli on top of the pasta if you have that sort of a pot; otherwise cook it in the microwave or in the conventional, old-fashioned, boil-the-hell-out-of-it way. Put the chicken in a big bowl, add pasta, baked vegetables, broccoli, mushrooms, chopped tomatoes, avocado, red pepper and spring onions. Add sea salt, freshly ground pepper and lashings of lemon juice and enjoy. Completely filling and completely low-fat — you can chop out the avocado if you have no life.

Chicken and Three Mushroom Risotto

Three sorts of mushrooms (or two, or even just one,
but make them big ones)
Chicken thighs or breast
Risotto or arborio rice
Lots of chicken stock
Lots of water

Stuff It!

Lots of lemon juice
Tiny bit of canola oil
Garlic
Salt and pepper

Put a tiny bit of oil, i.e. two teaspoonfuls, in the bottom of the pan and add the garlic. Cook a little bit and then add the rice. Stir this around and add the stock, preferably boiling. I use one of those little boxes that you buy in the supermarket. Keep stirring; the rice will soak up the stock. Add more water as it's soaked up. Chop the mushrooms and add to rice mixture. Keep adding water and stirring. Add salt and pepper and lemon juice (you may have noticed that I like lemon juice). When my husband makes this he adds the chicken into the rice mixture and cooks it at the same time as the mushrooms, but I prefer to grill the chicken in pieces, then chop it up and add it to the rice at the end, because I think it stays more tender that way. Of course, I can't tell him that. Oh no, siree. No way. His way is always the best way when it comes to the kitchen. In fact, the only reason I can share this with you now in the pages of this book is that I can guarantee he will not be reading this recipe because he already thinks he knows how to make this dish better than me. Hah! Risotto is cooked when you pop it in your mouth and it is soft and squishy. Believe me, it takes a lot of water. Probably four more of those little boxes that the stock came in. It may be an unusual colour, but this is a delicious chicken dinner and looks better if you serve it with a mixed, green-leaf salad and a balsamic vinegar dressing.

The other thing I do to try to stave off the hunger pangs — well, it would be a terrible thing to ever feel one of those would it not? — is have a big and bulky breakfast. I still have the breakfast they slopped, I mean served, up at Camp Eden. It actually takes some strength and courage to continue with this routine because if I eat it at work my mature and supportive colleagues yell, 'Oooh yuk, get that disgusting mess away from me,' and other similar taunts from the playground. I just love working with real professionals.

However, this breakfast makes you completely forget about food until lunchtime at the earliest because it settles like a rock in your stomach and refuses to make way for anything else.

Big and Bulky Breakfast

Jumbo rolled oats
Raisins
Dried apricots

Soak all the ingredients overnight in a bowl of water. Serve with lo-fat yoghurt or milk, and fresh fruit like bananas or kiwifruit, and/or tinned lo-cal fruit such as squishy peaches. Should those in the vicinity taunt you for persevering with this sometimes unsavoury-looking dish, simply flick bits of it at them and they will be forced to seek surgical help for its removal.

I always have three meals a day and I try to have a snack if I'm hungry so that I'm not holding out for dinner and eating myself into a stupor, even if it is a low-fat one.

I also try to drink 2 litres of water a day even though we all know water without sugar or any actual flavour added to it is as boring as bat shit. However, there seems to be a lot of research saying something or other about how it la-la-las your yadder-yadder-yadder so I get through eight glasses a day for those reasons.

Obviously, I am still 10 (yes, OK, possibly the 20 side of 10) kilos overweight so my system has some flaws, but this is how I have rid myself of the 20 kilos I am not under any circumstances having back about my person ever again, thank you very much for asking.

To lose the next 10 (yes, yes, or whatever), I need to increase the amount of exercise I do, probably to six times a week, because exercise really chips away at the kilos for me, even though I recognise it as the work of an evil force that will probably eventually take over the world. Well, how else do you explain all those abdominizer ads, hm?

I also need to cut down on the amount of food I eat, especially at dinner time. I would probably find this quite hard because what I have discovered post-fat farm is that feeling full is what makes me stop eating. Feeling full of healthy food is better than feeling full of cheeseburgers and fries, but feeling not quite full and not wanting to eat any more is better again. I'll get a grip on this one day when I'm not so busy.

I probably also need either to not eat out as much, or to be a lot fussier when I do. I always go for the thing on the menu that sounds the least fatty, for example, some pasta dishes that do not have cream or anything else that is obviously going to clog your arteries, but sometimes when this arrives in front of you it is swimming in oil.

I have, on occasion, sent such dishes back, because I think it is possible to overdose on the extra virgin. But most times, I have eaten it. Most times, too, and this would be one of the few happy ironies of dieting I have ever discovered, I have felt queasy afterwards. Once you have made a serious effort to cut fat from your diet your body kicks up bobsy-die when you try to bring it back. This, in turn, makes you more committed to keeping fat away. There now, wasn't that a lovely story?

The other thing I would do if I really wanted to lose those extra 5 (it's my book and I can make it up if I want to) kilos is cut out alcohol. After that, I would buy the most sensible brown walking shoes you have ever seen in your life and join the Carmelite nuns.

- 20 -
Sausage roll models

*In which the importance of watching
famous people get fat is explored*

DANGEROUSLY SHORT of inspiration for my chapter on role models,
I decided to go to the bookstore and blatantly steal ideas from
other fat people. My goodness it must be a long time since I bought
a book on fad dieting — the selection was a veritable smorgasbord!

I could go on the *Liver Cleansing Diet*, the Joanna Lumley *Bolly
and Stoli Diet*, The Lesley Kenton *Time-For-Another-Book-On-Diets
Diet*, I could still go on Rosemary Conley's *Hip and Thigh Diet*
(although I actually still have two copies of that at home), I can
go on the Roseanne *Screw Diets Try Liposuction Diet*, I can go on
the *Supermodels' Oxygen and H20 Diet* — why I can even *Be a Size
12 in 21 Days*.

Actually, that one came as a bit of a shock. Size 12 in 21 days?
I want to go on that diet. Now! I can drop a dress size a week and
be thin in time for tea. Hell, who would want to read a book on
Thin Thighs In 36 Years when they could be a size 12 in 21 days?
Not me, that's for sure. Perhaps I'd better go back to my day job.

Of course, on close inspection *Be a Size 12 in 21 Days* is actually
a book for underweight, 9-year-old Appalachian pygmies who
are, in fact, advised to spend three weeks at my house eating their
way up to a size 12. Oh well, I suppose that is more realistic.

Anyway, understandably overwhelmed by the heady selection of diet books, I suddenly found myself instead standing in front of the recipe books — well, the pictures are better! I put down Luther Van Dross's *Guide to Weight Maintenance* and picked up Delia Smith's *Winter Collection*; hang on, maybe Martha Stewart's *Recipes for Only Eating Pastel-Coloured Food* was a better buy? But what about *Low-fat Food Finnish-Style*, or *How To Get Your Mail-Order Bride To Cook A Fry-Up Just The Way You Like It*, or *99 Things To Do With Ketchup Apart From Putting It On Food?* My head was spinning. I was spoiled for choice. What to choose? What to choose? The pressure was too much — suddenly everything went black.

Next thing I knew I was sitting in the bookshop coffee bar where all they had left was sausage rolls and custard squares. I had one of each.

Oh, who needs role models anyway?

Actually, I was deeply upset to read that Elizabeth Taylor had started exercising at the ripe old age of just-about-to-turn-65. I have long relied on Liz to be a role model to the curvaceous, and news that she had employed a personal trainer and was power-walking through her own personal track in the Hollywood Hills hit me like a smack in the face with a wet piece of pizza.

Liz, how could you? All those years of ballooning and deflating reassured millions of women the globe over that not only was it an acceptable thing to do but something that could even be considered stylish and endearing, and better still, could be squeezed in between marrying and divorcing husbands. You don't think stretch caftans would have been a big hit on their own, do you Liz? Without you, they're nothing.

I have always imagined Liz sitting at home in her velour pantsuit eating Kentucky Fried Chicken out of a huge bucket while watching re-runs of *National Velvet* and 'Lassie' on cable television. In fact, I've always thought it strange her perfumes do not smell more like pizza as I had been lead to believe that this was her true essence. Well, I'd buy it. And wear it.

Stuff It!

Has Elizabeth Taylor's battle of the bulge ever mattered to anyone apart from herself? Not a jot. Liz Taylor could've been the size of Houston and Richard Burton would still have loved her and married her and left her and loved her and married her again. Her struggle with her erratic weight has been witnessed all around the world, but no one's ever given up on her or decided that she wasn't beautiful or bewitching because of it. OK, so that picture on the front of *Hollywood Babylon* didn't help but, hey, by the time the picture was developed she'd probably halved her hip measurement, anyway. And never mind her bulging belly and flubbery thighs — have you ever noticed that no matter how round she gets, she still has the most fabulous neck and shoulders, and boy does she make the most of them? That's the secret.

It's quite comforting, too, don't you find, that money can't actually make you thin on its own? I mean, here's Liz with literally hundreds of millions of dollars lying around and she still has to haul her own buns up and down a string of boring old hills to fit them into her caftans. So, she can hire a tanned, gay man called Purcell to shout, 'C'mon, Ms Taylor, you can do it, I know you can, and afterwards I'll make you some pukeschtick tea for purity,' but when it comes down to it — it's her own brain having to send messages to her own muscles in her own legs to get them moving.

At the end of the day, she probably avoids looking in mirrors when she's having a fat day and sits on the end of her bed crying because none of her rhinestone-encrusted ball gowns will do up — just like the rest of us. She probably sticks hat pins in voodoo dolls of Purcell, and wills him to get that job he really wants doing cereal commercials so he'll get off her back and leave her to lie on her heart-shaped, velour waterbed. She probably looks back at photos of herself when she was in *Cleopatra* and cries, 'I'd give the tops of my legs to be that fat now!'

She's one of us.

I had thought that Sarah Ferguson, the Duchess of York was one of us, too. Looking through her photo albums from when she started life as a chubby, Janet Frame lookalike to when she slimmed down for her wedding and fattened up for her divorce would certainly give one cause for thinking so. Interesting how one talks so much more about one when one discusses royalty, doesn't one? I've always been a Fergie sympathiser because she's been quite open about how miserable her fatness made her when she was married to Prince Andrew, especially when those nasty British tabloids started calling her the Duchess of Pork.

The poor dear was never helped by her choice of clothing, either and frankly, whoever was advising her should have been relieved of their head in the time-honoured tradition. You should have stuck with black, Fergie, and since brown is the new black, brown, and since navy is the new brown, navy. When one knows one is being trailed by hundreds of scum-of-the-earth paparazzi and one correspondingly hates one's cellulite being on the front page (oops, wrong daughter-in-law), one should steer clear of large patterns and gathered skirts, that's the harsh reality of being in the flashlight.

When I read Fergie's autobiography I felt truly sorry for her because she didn't like being known around the world as a frumpy fatty — well, who would? I also felt deeply resentful of her because she first started putting on weight at boarding school and used to console herself on visits home by rushing straight to the Aga, cooking up a dozen sausages at a pop and nibbling on them through the hour, while Dads was no doubt upstairs availing himself of the parlour maid. After reading that do you think I could get the thought of hot, sizzling snarlers out of my mind? Not until I'd eaten two or three fresh off the griller myself, and I swear I still have a lump on my thigh that sprang up that day as a result.

Poor Fergie bemoans the fact that while the Duke of York was off at sea she didn't even have a kitchen in the rat-and-cockroach-infested hovel she called Buckingham Palace, and she had to rely on some ancient old retainer to wobble up from the kitchen, literally a mile away, with whatever was on the menu that day.

Presumably she could also order up crates of salt and vinegar crisps and her own weight in Mars Bars, too.

Therefore, I was intrigued to see, in early 1997, that Fergie had been named the spokesperson for the American Weightwatchers group. This was part of a very lucrative deal aimed at knocking a chunk off her multi-million pound overdraft — (other gems of which included the I Slept With Fergie For a Tenner T-shirts that nanna brought home from her London Shoppe tour of the British Isles). Fergie doesn't actually mention anything about Weightwatchers in her book, but I'm sure that doesn't mean she's fibbing when she says joining the group was instrumental in trimming down from Fat Frumpy Freebie Fun-loving Fergie to the slim-line Sarah Ferguson.

Anyway, no sooner had the announcement of her appointment been made than Fergie was quoted as saying she had put her 'chunky' eight-year-old daughter, Princess Beatrice, on a diet after seeing her in her swimming togs. No more bread, chips or fizzy drinks for you, Fergie told her daughter.

All I can say is that if Fergie ate because she was made to feel inadequate by her parents I'd put money on the future of Meaty, Beefy, Big and Bouncy Beatrice. Lucky little princess, having her mummy describe her to the world as 'chunky'. What a jolly jape that is!

Why didn't Fergie just quietly cut down on Big Bea's chippies and fizzy drinks, and provide her with interesting, healthy alternatives herself (OK, we all know there is no such thing, but what about bribing her with trinkets, then)? It's not like Beatrice is popping down to New World for her own supplies, after all. Now she knows she is fat. Great, big, bummer, Beatrice. Her mother should have known better, and I hope she doesn't make a big deal out of seeing her eldest daughter in her togs ever again. The last thing the world needs is another neurotic princess. Next thing she'll be throwing herself down cheesegraters and vomiting into her squash bag like her famous auntie, Diana ('What — call that cellulite? Are you drunk?'), Princess of Wales.

I think one of the best role models young New Zealanders have is Rachel Hunter. She may be as thick as a plank, but you can't deny she's as cunning as a fox when it comes to money; she has great wodges of it lying around all over the place by most accounts. Of course, she's no Mama Cass, but for a supermodel she is beefy and proud of it. (However, after one photo shoot her New Zealand manager did try to pass off little bits of Rachel's flab as 'too much muscle definition', and said the pictures were not to be used!) Not for our Rach the gaunt face and chiselled cheekbones of Linda, Kate and Christy. No, here's a supermodel who has sweaty armpits, and probably has been known to have the odd bit of chaffing between the thighs. She's got all the right curves in all the right places, and she's a happy, healthy, working mum and our very own royalty — without the vomiting, toe-sucking, cheesegrating, Squidgygating, etc., etc., etc., of course.

To be honest, I know I suffer from an addiction to TV chat shows, but I think Oprah Winfrey has done a pretty good job of getting off her big old butt and getting rid of her big old butt. The second time, of course.

I do possess a copy of *Making The Connection*, the book Oprah wrote with her trainer Bob Greene, and I have to say that while it's nowhere near as good — and I'm sure you will agree with me — as this book, it's pretty good, nonetheless.

At her heftiest, Oprah weighed 237 pounds, and it's morbidly fascinating to read how even though she's the richest entertainer in America and the number one in her field, she still felt like a big bag of iguana droppings, the way we all do when we know our eating is out of control. For us, of course, it might be that we feel embarrassed getting out of the car or climbing the stairs at work. For Oprah, it was sitting in the front row at the Emmy Awards, hoping against hope that her name wouldn't be read out as the winner because then she'd have to get out of her chair and waddle up on stage, revealing the enormity of her behind!

Isn't it just the meanest thing ever that you can be the best in the whole wide world at something and worth an immense fortune, but your fat legs make you hate yourself and feel totally worthless? Frankly, the whole system stinks, and in a perfect world, fat wouldn't even have a name it would be so unimportant. If only that were the case I would be lying on the sofa right now watching Harrison Ford movies and eating cheezel sandwiches. But, as they say at Camp Eden, if only is, um, a bad thing and shouldn't be something-or-other, which I'm sure you've all heard before.

Identifying with a famous person, though, somehow does make the struggle a bit easier for us regular fat folk. You know, Oprah even passed up going to a party at Don Johnson's house in Aspen once because she felt too fat and had nothing to wear. How many times have you done that? Not passed up an invite to Don Johnson's, of course, but to anywhere else because you just felt too darned fat? Naturally, if I was invited to Don Johnson's house for a party I think I could manage to put my fatness behind me (what do you mean there's already enough there?) for a minute or two, and just check out the decor and perhaps see what Melanie — is he back with her yet? — can do with a canapé.

Oprah felt much worse about this fat because she had already gotten rid of it once by drinking diet juice for four months and was down to her old size 10 jeans. The moment she got back on to real food, though, the weight came back. Yep, that old chestnut. And no matter how many millions of dollars she had, she couldn't keep the new fat from coming back.

So Oprah takes her big old butt to an American version of Camp Eden, and there she meets Bob Greene and waddya know, she likes the guy so much she buys him! This is where your and my stories would differ from Oprah's, but at least she's been good enough to let us ride on the back of success by spelling out its formula in *Make the Connection*, which offers up a pretty sensible ten-step plan to permanent weight loss, and has the benefit of lots of fat photos of Oprah and excerpts from the diary she kept when she was still eating New York.

Bob basically told Oprah that eating low-fat food was not enough if she was serious about losing weight and keeping it off; she needed to exercise, preferably every day, for at least 20 minutes at a very intense level — and eat low-fat food.

Oprah's money came in quite handy here because she ordered herself in a special chef who made all her meals and she started taking Bob with her everywhere, even on holiday, so he could boss her into working out every morning, even if it meant getting up at 4.30 a.m. The key for her has been making exercise a normal part of her day, rather than tacking it on as the really yukky thing at the end.

Oprah has stuck with her regime for three years in a row and has not regained any of her old fat. However, it hasn't all been plain sailing. As her weight dropped, her ratings looked like doing the same. How's that for cruel irony? The viewers wanted the fat old Oprah, not the skinny new one! One woman even came on the show and admitted that she had once dreamed of having Oprah over for dinner but that now she was skinny, she didn't even want Oprah to drop by!

Bitch! I bet Oprah never wanted to go to her house anyway.

But that does bring us round to the whole point of trying to please people. I can remember a school friend of mine saying to me once, 'Oh don't get thin — you wouldn't be you', which gave me a pretty good excuse to high-tail it straight down to Victoria market and buy a bag of home-made chocolate fudge and coconut ice, which is what she wanted to do all along, only not on her own. She was thin.

When you have a reputation as an enthusiastic winer and diner, it can be hard to turn down invitations from the people who like wining and dining with you. These are usually very good and close friends whom you love and adore but who probably do not have a weight problem. They also probably love you the way you are and don't even notice that you only ever wear baggy shirts in colours that make it difficult to see you at night, and that when they are all going to the beach you are always strangely stricken down with a mystery virus not dissimilar to the sort of thing Michael Jackson might go to Switzerland to get treatment for. But when you are trying to change your eating habits and they are desperate to try the newest anything-that-moves-deep-fry-it restaurant, saying no can take a lot of willpower, and it may well be willpower you already used up staying at the office having the lunch you brought instead of going to the park for fish and chips with the other girls.

I suffer from a great fear of disappointing people (no big deal, it's a Catholic thing), and I often go out eating and drinking when I would really feel a whole lot better doing something that doesn't involve starting every conversation with 'I think I'll have… Don't get me wrong — it's not like it's torture or anything, I absolutely love eating out — it just doesn't make me feel the best I can feel. I also find it very hard to eat out and find food that fits in with the low-fat regime I try to be on, especially when every single place these days seems to specialise in pizza and in a cruel genetic twist I am fatally attracted to anything made of dough and covered in cheese and other delicacies. The thing is, if you want to eat out and fall off the wagon, you should — and suffer the consequences. (Oh, my God, it's the ghost of Sister Eulalia. I swear I didn't type those words myself.)

But it's better to do it for you than because someone else is begging you to help them have a good time, because at the end of the day, it's your hips that will never wriggle into a pair of Levi's, not theirs.

Honestly, your real friends are still your friends whether you're sharing nachos (extra cheese, please!) with them or going for a walk along the beach with them, and what I try to do now is not keep my weight such a secret from the people I hang out with, especially the skinny ones. It's much easier to keep on the straight and narrow when you have the support of those around you.

In fact, I'm thinking of getting Temuera Morrison to front a campaign aimed at stopping people from forcing sausage rolls on their friends when it's obvious they have already had enough. This advertising campaign will be so successful it will be made into a movie called *Once Were Weightwatchers* in which a dysfunctional family go on a fish and chip and swearing binge until the mother gets campylobacter from a dud oyster and loses so much weight she decides to start up her own health farm exclusively for gang members with symmetrical facial tattoos.

On the proceeds of this Oscar-winning feature film, I will fly to Chicago and head-hunt Oprah's special cook and her trainer Bob Greene, because although it's great to know rich fat people have the same problems, what we all really want to know is what it's like to have their solutions.

- 21 -
The heavier side of dieting

In which the whole point of outing yourself as a fatso is explained

━━━━━

IT IS NOT ALWAYS EASY to see the lighter side of dieting because sometimes there simply isn't one, and anyone who doesn't measure up to their own expectations when it comes to how they look, knows this.

I'm not necessarily talking about people who've had to make their dresses out of old army tents, either. Sometimes, being 4 kilos overweight feels just as stink as being 44 (kilos that is; as far as I know there is nothing wrong with being 44 years of age).

The point is that rather than continuing wringing our hands and gnashing our teeth over our extra pounds, we should lower our expectations. I can honestly say from personal experience that being big is not the worst thing that a person can be — far from it.

It's much better than being stupid or boring. It's much better than being nasty or dishonest. It's certainly much better than being the sort of person who drives in the fast lane even though you're only doing 60 kilometres an hour and will you *please* move out of the way… Yes. Well. Compared to a lot of other things you can be, carrying a few extra kilos is practically a gift. Why do we make it such a big deal?

Truthfully? It is probably better to be thin and jolly than fat and jolly, but since I've never been thin and jolly at the same time, this is hard to verify. I'm sure that given the fact that the world currently bears an irritating and unfair intolerance towards the plump, not being plump would make life simpler and easier. And if I rubbed a bottle and a genie popped out, my first wish would be to have a body like Elle McPherson. My second wish would be a lifetime supply of kettle fry crisps of assorted flavours. And my third wish would be that I could consume my second wish without any fear of ruining my first wish.

But back here in the real world, I'm never going to get my first wish. With the help of corporate sponsorship I might get the second, but without the third let's face it, I'm looking at a nightmare, not a dream come true.

I know that a magic wand is never going to be waved over my hips and thighs. I know there is no miracle diet that is going to get me into a size 12. I have tried every diet known to Western civilisation, aside from famine, and in the 25 years I have been on these diets, I have put on weight.

It's time to back the truth truck up and unload.

The person inside the pounds is a much bigger deal than the pounds themselves, but no skinny person is going to believe that until we believe it ourselves.

We all have to face the fact that being Elle McPherson is such a hard job that really only one person can succeed at it, and God only knows how many hours she spends on the exercycle and what chemicals she ingests just to keep that job. It must be Elle!

And even Elle probably has fat days. Probably not as many since the liposuction. Oh, did I not mention the liposuction?

I was delighted in the way that only a weight-watcher can be to learn the other day that the gorgeous lead singer of an American rock and roll band had fat days, too.

'I'll be walking through a club thinking, I'm so fat today,' admitted whippet-thin Gwen Stefani, the blonde bombshell who fronts No Doubt. 'And then this girl comes up and says, "You're so beautiful. Can I have your autograph?" And it's like, If you only knew what's going through my head right now! Thanks for coming up and saving me from, like, slaughtering myself.' For all I know she probably weighs 150 kilos and is married to Michael Jackson, but I still, like, like where she is coming from.

You see, if people who won't wear clothes unless they reveal their navels can have fat days, why shouldn't fat people have them? Why try to be as thin as them when it's obvious you never will be and what would be the point anyway because you'd probably still be sitting on the end of your bed blubbing and wailing, 'All these ribbons of lycra and nothing in bla-a-a-a-a-ack'?

I've been fat and I've been thin and neither was better. Being happy is better. And being happy means taking off all your clothes, looking in the mirror, and saying, 'OK, you have a baggy, fat suit on — but I like you.' I've had to come to terms with the fact that I will never be thin again. I will never be as fat as I was again either, because my expectations of myself are now realistic so I am not going to fail dismally in my bid to wear Kylie Minogue's cast-offs, thus thrusting myself into a deep depression, followed by a quick decision to give up all hope and move into a caravan in the carpark at KFC.

The me I am now has a wonderful husband, a loving family, the best of friends, and after 35 years, a pair of thighs that may not be thin, but I can live with.

A year after I got back from my life-changing torture treatment in the depths of the Queensland rainforest, I went into a jeans shop and I bought a pair of Levi's.

I cannot count how many conversations I have had with overweight women whose goal is to 'get back into a pair of jeans'. The humble denim pant is a symbol of being just like all the other girls, and the feeling you get when you can button up a pair over your tummy without them playing havoc with your chances of procreation is like no other I can recall.

The day I bought those jeans, I got to just outside the shop and started umming and ahhing about even darkening the doorstep, despite the fact Mark and I had made a special trip to that very shop for that very purpose.

Cajoled inside, I went through my usual routine of surreptitiously checking out the biggest sizes and freezing with panic whenever a stick figure approached me to ask if I needed any help. I refused all help. I did not want some waif-like strumpet knowing my waist measurement. I was keeping it a secret!

Finally, armed with a variety of the largest pairs I could find, I snuck into the changing rooms, making sure Mark was stationed right outside to ward off any unwanted intrusions.

Here I was having yet another sweaty moment in yet another sweaty changing room. Could I handle it if these bloody jeans didn't fit? Would I be catapulted into a frenzy of double flame-grilled whoppers at the Burger King across the road if the buttons strained across my tummy without meeting each other? Bugger it, I thought, and pulled the first pair on. They didn't fit. Neither did the second pair. Neither did the third.

At this stage, Mark was beginning to look decidedly nervous. He had lived with me long enough to realise that as it had been his idea to come all this way to get a pair of jeans, it would therefore be his fault that the mission had proved impossible. Intervention, he decided at this stage and clearly without my permission, was the key. A stick insect was brought in.

'Oh, those are no good,' she smiled, ignoring my horrified face as she snatched the piles of denim from the floor. 'You want the 515s. I'll be right back.' What I really wanted, of course, was for her to be 6 stone heavier and covered in acne, but instead I got a pair of 515s.

Glaring at my husband — who was hiding behind the Hawaiian shirt collection — I pulled the jeans over my hips. I did up the buttons. I did not suck in my stomach. I was not being cut in half. I was wearing a pair of jeans. You have never seen the zip zap of a credit card move so quickly. I was practically in shock.

The moment we got in the door at home I put those jeans straight on, and cried. All the months of passing up pies and pastries and pina coladas flashed before my eyes, and right then and there I realised it was *so* worth it. It is a moment I will never forget, and I don't care if the arse falls out of those jeans and you can count every ripple of my cellulite, I will never, ever part with them and I will always, always fit them. Even if I have to tie them between two horses and stretch the bejeezus out of them.

Tears and laughter have played an important part through the pages of this book, and although the objective has been to examine the dieting issue from the ridiculous viewpoint it so richly deserves, I haven't always been able to laugh because it hasn't always been a laughing matter.

I feel sad when I think of myself at 17, standing on the scales and cursing them because I just couldn't get down to 9 stone.

I feel sad when I think of myself at 33, standing on the scales and cursing them because I was in to triple figures!

I feel sad that in the years between those two moments I have wasted so much time sweating the small stuff — which is exactly what extra weight is, only bigger, of course.

I should've been worrying about world peace, not thin thighs! OK, so I stole that off a Miss America contestant, but you know what I mean. A bit of flubber hanging around your midriff is not enough of an excuse to feel bad about yourself. Being overweight is not enough of an excuse for hanging back or not doing everything you can do. Sure, you can use it as an excuse if you're short of others, but just don't start believing it.

I have had to really push myself in my life to do things that I did not want to do because I have been afraid that people would find out I was fat. It has been my weak point.

When I was asked to be the editor of the *New Zealand Woman's*

Weekly, I never doubted my ability to identify with New Zealand women, produce a magazine, or manage a team of 30 people. I worried about being fat. After all, there's only so much that wearing black can disguise.

When I was asked to co-host a radio breakfast show, I never doubted that I could spin a good yarn, make people laugh or get up at 4.30 in the morning. I worried about being fat. And I don't even have a particularly fat voice.

But now that I have outed myself as a lard-arse, you know what? I don't have a weak point any more.

Just recently I was described in a national newspaper as a 'media heavyweight' in an article headlined something like 'Why looky here, a great big fat bastard has done something mildly interesting', or was it 'Weight lent to media training'? The story was about a media training company I have with set up with three friends in various parts of the industry, and was accompanied by a photo which obviously prompted the hilarious headline and jaunty weight-related jibe. This time last year, I would have laid down on my bed and wept because some spotty youth who wouldn't be a journalist's arsehole had pegged me as a heffalump. Yesterday, I thought, 'Cool, free publicity.' I'm making my fat work for me from now on.

Some people have looked at me in horror when I've told them I'm writing a book on the subject. 'Why on earth would you want to do a thing like that?' they've asked, their mouths agape. And frankly, as long as people gawk at me disbelievingly while flies inhabit their molars, wondering why I am going public about being fat, I feel pretty happy that I have. Why shouldn't I? That's the whole point. What's so wrong with being fat? If I'd reared lesbian love triplets or eaten only cocktail sausages for 24 years, nobody would think twice about it, but admit publicly that your thighs are wobbly and dimply and *'Oh my God! Have you thought about the consequences?'*

Well, yes, I have thought about the consequences.

Stuff It!

The consequences are that now everybody is going to know I am fat. The ones that didn't pick it up on the *New Zealand Woman's Weekly* TV ads, that is. The ones that didn't read about it in the country's best-read magazine. The ones that didn't hear me talk about it on the radio. Yes, they'll all know the embarrassing truth now. I eat too much and I don't exercise enough. It's true.

But I'm still healthy and I'm still happy. And if I can make one tiny little bit of difference in the world (apart from inventing no-risk slimming tablets that look, feel and taste like kettle fry crisps — I'm still working on that, too), I would like at least one nine-year-old, teenager, working girl, young mum, or old-age bowling champ to read this book, forget their fat day, hitch up their elastic waistband, look the world in the eye and say, 'Stuff it!'.

- 22 -
The oh-my-God-she's-a-blob-again disclaimer

In which the author covers her butt
should it treble in size

IF, THE NEXT TIME you see me, I am getting the front of my house pulled down so that 22 firemen can lift me on to a crane and get me to the hospital on the back of a truck for heart surgery, please disregard chapters 18, 19 and 21.

Also, could you please make sure the firemen have a nice hot cup of tea (best drink of the day) and plenty of gingernuts. It's really not the sort of job they should be doing on an empty stomach.

The End.